JOB

A Study in Providence and Faith

by Ralph L. Smith

Convention Press
NASHVILLE • TENNESSEE

© Copyright 1971 • Convention Press
Nashville, Tennessee

All rights reserved
5132-10

Dewey Decimal classification number: 221.1
Printed in the United States of America

Preface

IT IS HIGHLY APPROPRIATE and perhaps providential that the book of Job has been chosen for study at this particular time. This book speaks to our present situation as few others do. Our lives, like Job's, are often fraught with problems, frustrations, suffering, hostilities, and fear. Many people in our time are asking questions Job must have asked: Is there any meaning to life? Is there an overruling Providence capable of bringing good out of evil, joy out of sadness, fruition and finality out of the frustrations and failures of the past and present? The book of Job answers these questions with an unequivocal yes. The overruling Providence is the Creator and Redeemer, and that which gives meaning to life is the fact that man is a part of a divine purpose that cannot be thwarted (42:2).

Sufferers find in the book of Job a word of encouragement. Suffering may come upon one suddenly, mercilessly, and inexplicably. We, like Job, may never know why we are suffering. We may never receive a rational or theological explanation for it, but we can be sure that God will give us grace enough to bear it.

There is a word of warning here for the dogmatist who would jump too quickly to God's defense and, on the basis of a too mechanical application of an inherited creed, condemn an innocent sufferer.

There is likewise a word of warning here for the impatient, idealistic, young person such as Elihu, who thinks that the older generation has failed miserably and that there are simple solutions to the world's complicated problems.

There is a word of instruction here for the one who is preoccupied with ethics. Perhaps the highest standard of ethical conduct for an individual is set out in Job 31. (See chap. 8 of this study guide.)

The purpose of this study book is to guide the reader through the book of Job so that its message will come through. It is not intended to be a substitute for the book of Job. The biblical book is primary, and the student who reads this study guide without reading the book of Job will fail to gain maximum understanding. An attempt is made to supply background materials, outlines, and linguistic and theological analyses that will make it easier for the reader to understand and interpret Job.

How does one study a book such as Job? By themes or by characters? There are various ways such a study can be made. I have chosen to deal with the material exactly as it is presented in the book itself. I have followed the natural outline of the book. I could have rearranged the material for our study, but the result would more than likely have been Smith's version rather than the Spirit's version.

I would like to express my gratitude to Howard Colson, editorial secretary of the Sunday School Board, for the invitation to write this study guide, and to Ernest L. Hollaway and Mavis Allen for their counsel and assistance in editing the material. I would also like to thank Vivian Wallace for typing the original manuscript.

Fort Worth, Texas RALPH L. SMITH

Available for

January Bible Study, 1972

Tried and True

The Book of Job in

Today's English Version

Prepared and released by
American Bible Society

This inexpensive printing of the new translation of Job will be helpful both in the promotion and the conducting of the special annual Bible study. Copies may be ordered by title and number (04450) from your Baptist Book Store or the American Bible Society, Box 5656, Grand Central Station, New York, New York 10017

Workbook for Job—A Study in Providence and Faith

The workbook will provide guidelines for reading, understanding, and applying the Bible and the factual material contained in the January Bible Study book for the study of Job. To the extent that it is possible in this format, this workbook will provide a "program" of self-instruction. The workbook will be useful for individual study, for class preparation, even for use in a class session; but its content primarily will be self-help Bible study material.

John B. Doherty, supervisor, engineering section, property management staff, Sunday School Board, Nashville, Tennessee prepared the workbook.

Teaching Guide for Job—A Study in Providence and Faith

The teaching guide will contain preparation helps and teaching aids for each chapter of the January Bible Study book on Job. It will integrate into one set of teaching suggestions the other materials provided for use with the January Bible Study on Job. It will suggest resource books and visual aids to be used by teachers. It will offer alternate proposals for the teacher who wishes to be more—or less—innovative in his teaching.

The writer is J. Thomas Trimble, chairman, department of psychology, Belmont College, Nashville, Tennessee.

Table of Contents

1

Introduction:

Interpreting the Book of Job

LAVISH PRAISE has been heaped upon the book of Job. Martin Luther described it as "magnificent and sublime." Tennyson called it "the greatest poem of ancient or modern times." Carlyle said, "I call it . . . one of the grandest things ever written . . . a noble book; all men's book! There is nothing written, I think, in the Bible or out of it of equal literary merit." C. F. Kent referred to Job as "the Matterhorn of the Old Testament." H. H. Rowley said, "That the book of Job is the supreme literary masterpiece in the Old Testament and one of the greatest creations of the world's religions is generally agreed."[1]

A Great Book

To what should we attribute the greatness of the book of Job? Any literary masterpiece must have beauty and sharpness of language, an engaging form and style that is well executed, and a theme that is enduring and universal. Job has all three of these qualities in abundance.

The book of Job contains some of the most beautiful and picturesque expressions in all literature: "the eyelids of the morning" (41:18); "the skin of my teeth" (19:20); "Is there any taste in the white of an egg?" (6:6); "who giveth songs in the night" (35:10); and "the doors of his face" (41:14).

Job has the style and form of a masterpiece. It has suspense and graphic descriptions; it contains word plays, innuendoes, metaphors, similes, and makes much use of irony. The work of Job is great partly because of the literary skill which produced it.

Job is great because it has an enduring and universal theme, one that touches our common humanity and one which the passing of the years cannot alter. Its theme is the unexplained presence of suffering in the world. However, it is not just the theme that makes Job great; it is the satisfying conclusion which the book offers. The solution of the problem of suffering is not found in the Satanism, pantheism, nihilism, or atheism that have been common in our times. Job's solution to the problem of suffering is found in a staunch belief that God, the Creator, is both just and sovereign.

Above all, the book of Job is great because it is the inspired Word of God. While the literary skill of the author would serve to make it a great book, the enduring quality of Job—its ultimate greatness—is the result of divine inspiration. It is holy Scripture and should be understood as such.

A Fascinating Book

The book of Job has a fascination about it that has attracted the attention of writers, artists, and the common man through the centuries. Goethe (1749–1832) patterned his most famous work *Faust* on the book of Job. William Blake in 1825 published twenty-one watercolor drawings illustrating the high points of the book of Job. These drawings represent Blake's enthusiasm for the book and his unusual interpretation of it.

George Bernard Shaw criticized the book of Job in *Black Girl in Search of God.* Robert Frost, in *A Masque of Reason,* chides God for carrying out the Joban experiment. At the close of the poem he says: "Here endeth chapter forty-three of Job."

But the modern writer who has done most to call attention to the book of Job is Archibald MacLeish. MacLeish's play *J.B.* had a long run on Broadway in the late nineteen fifties. In the play a man named J.B. is successful in business, has a nice family, and is outwardly religious. Then tragedy overtakes him. His oldest son, who had been in the army, is killed (after the war is over) through a careless officer's mistake. News of the son's death is brought to J.B. and his wife Sarah by two drunken GI's.

Two more of J.B.'s children are killed in an automobile accident, and his youngest daughter is raped and murdered by a psychopath. J.B.'s bank is destroyed by a bombing in which his last child dies. J.B.'s health breaks, and his wife deserts him. Three friends, a psychiatrist, a politician, and a minister come to see him. They, like their biblical counterparts, are miserable comforters, though for a different reason. They will not let J.B. be guilty. According to them there is no justice in the universe, and where all are guilty, none are guilty. The only solution J.B. finds is in human love. J.B. forgives God and concludes that all of the candles in the churches have gone out. The "coals of the heart" are all the light that is left! What a dark picture!

MacLeish, like many moderns, knew about the book of Job, but he either missed its message or was unable to accept its solution as his own. According to MacLeish, man is left to his own fate. He has no resources other than his own. How different are the words of Job: "I know that my Redeemer liveth," and "I had heard of thee with the hearing of the ear, but now my eye sees thee!" *J.B.* is humanism pure and simple, yet it captures much of the crisis and pathos of our age.

The message of Job is attractive to the modern reader. It speaks of intense and unexplained suffering to an age that has known Auschwitz, Hiroshima, and Vietnam. It cries out against the injustices and inequities of life to an age torn by riots, bombings, and burning. It protests against shallow and inadequate answers to ultimate questions in an age that has had its "God is dead" advocates. Job recounts a search for meaning, and it offers a solution.

How to Interpret the Book

It is easier to praise the book of Job than to understand it. Scholars are almost unanimous in their praise of the book, but there is wide disagreement among them concerning its origin and meaning. Because of its wide acclaim, Job has become a classic. But classics have a way of being neglected. (Mark Twain defined a classic as "something that everybody wants to have read and nobody wants to read.") This has been the fate of Job in far too many cases. Genuine praise of the book must be based on firsthand knowledge, and such knowledge can come only through diligent study.

The Difficulty of the Task

Job is not an easy book to read. It is hard to read, first, because it is old. Its language is old. Its customs and concepts are old; and, therefore, they appear strange. We no longer speak of such things as Leviathan (41:1) or the heavenly council (1:6; 2:1).

Job is hard to read because it is poetry (great poetry, but poetry, nonetheless). Poetic expressions are often hard to grasp. In this busy and pragmatic age, few people have time or concern for poetry. To understand the book of Job, one must be able to appreciate great poetry and be willing to give time and thought to its words.

Again, the book of Job is hard to read because it is theological and philosophical. It deals with some of the ultimate questions of life: Why was I born (3:3; 10:18)? Why serve God (1:9)? Can a man be righteous before God (4:17)? Can a man by searching find out the deep things of God (11:7)? If a man die, shall he live again (14:14)? Can a man be profitable to God (22:2)? Is it any pleasure to the Almighty that one is righteous (22:3)? These and other questions probe the deep issues of life. They call for thought and involvement from the reader.

Finally, the book of Job is hard to read because of the inadequacy of many of our English translations. Job is very hard to translate. Jerome told of his struggles with this book while he was making his translation for the Vulgate. He said that it was "slippery as an eel." He told how he engaged at no small cost a Jewish teacher from Lydda, who had a great reputation but who failed to throw much light on the book. Jerome confessed sadly that after the teacher had gone through it with him he was no wiser than before.

Job is especially hard to translate because its vocabulary is unusual. Many words in the text of Job do not occur anywhere else in the Hebrew Bible, and many of these words occur only one time in Job. The text is so obscure in places that some scholars have argued that the book was originally written in Arabic or Aramaic and translated into Hebrew.

If one desires to understand the book of Job today, he should read it in as many modern versions as possible. Some of the more recent translations of the Old Testament and Job are: the Revised Standard Version, The New English Bible, Moffatt's translation, Smith and Goodspeed's translations, the Anchor Bible, the Jerusalem Bible, and the New American Standard Version of the Old Testament to be published in the near future.[2] (*Except where otherwise indicated, the Revised Standard Version is used in this study guide.*)

The American Bible Society has just released, in a special printing timed to be used with this study, the book of Job in *Today's English Version.* (See p. v for information on ordering.)

The Need for Objectivity

If the book of Job is to speak to us today we must let it say what *it* says, not what we want it to say or think it should say. If at times Job charges God with injustice, as he seems to do in 9:22–24 and 21:22–26, we must understand what he says and come to terms with it. If some of Job's words appear to be blasphemy, we must not try to soften them or alter them as the rabbis did. For example, very early the rabbis changed the reading of 7:20 from, "Why have I become a burden to thee?" to "Why have I become a burden to myself?" because in their minds no one could be a burden to God. (Compare KJV and RSV on this verse.) They also changed the reading of 32:3 from "they condemned God" to "they condemned Job."[3]

But the rabbis are not the only ones who have changed texts or who have held on to traditional readings which have been proved incorrect. One example in our English Bibles is the famous verse in 13:15, "Though he slay me, yet will I trust in him" (KJV). The Revised Standard Version (hereafter referred to as RSV) reads, "Behold, he will slay me; I have no hope." The RSV translation is from the Hebrew text, whereas the King James translators followed a reading in the margin of the Hebrew text.

Perhaps you are saying, "This is too technical and complicated for me." Perhaps so. But this is what we mean when we say we must let the Bible say what it says and not what we want it to say. If we change the text or translation to suit ourselves, we are practicing ventriloquism. In that case, it is not the Bible that is speaking; we are simply talking to ourselves. We are guilty of doing what Deuteronomy 4:2; 12:32 and Revelation 22:18–19 forbid: adding to or taking away from the Word of God. Job accused his three friends of speaking falsely for God (13:7). If we make the Bible say something it does not say, we "speak falsely for God."

There are certain basic rules or principles of interpretation which can help us avoid mistakes in understanding and which will allow the Bible to say what it says: the literary or grammatical principle, the historical principle, and the theological principle.[4] Every conscientious interpreter of the Word of God should give serious consideration to the use of these principles.

The Literary Principle

The literary principle is concerned with the language of the book as well as the style and form of writing. The language of the book of Job contains many rare words and unusual sentence structures. Part of the book is prose and part of it is poetry. The prose sections are: the prologue (1:1 to 2:13); the introduction to Elihu's speech (32:1–5); and the epilogue (42:7–17). The remainder of the book is poetry.

What is the difference between prose and poetry? Poetry is usually written in definite lines, as we see in the Revised Standard Version and other recent translations. It is marked by emotional and imaginative language, exalted diction, and regular rhythm. Prose is usually matter-of-fact narrative. It may be descriptive, parabolic, historical, or biographical. In prose, words are usually to be taken at their face value. Other factors should be taken into account when one is reading biblical poetry. For instance, one should not press the literal meaning of all poetic expressions, as in the case of "the morning stars sang together" (38:7). The language of the poetry of Job is exalted, emotional, imaginative; and it moves in regular rhythm.

One distinctive feature of Hebrew poetry is parallelism. Often the two lines of a verse will say the same thing in different words. This is called synonymous parallelism.

The book of Job is filled with this type of writing:

> By the breath of God they perish,
>   and by the blast of his anger they are consumed.
> —4:9

> Can mortal man be righteous before God?
>   Can a man be pure before his maker?
> —4:17

> For he wounds, but he binds up;
>   he smites, but his hands heal.
> —5:18

For other examples of synonymous parallelism, see also 6: 11, 12, 17, 19; 7:1, 2; 8:3, 11, 14.

Another type of parallelism, antithetic parallelism, is very common in the book of Proverbs but rare in Job. In this type of poetry, the second line expresses the opposite thought of the first line.

> A wise son makes a glad father,
>   but a foolish son is a sorrow to his mother
> —Proverbs 10:1

Some examples of antithetic parallelism in Job are 22:29; 36:6.

A third type of parallelism in Hebrew poetry is synthetic parallelism, in which the second line completes the thought of the first line. Many examples of this type are found in Job, for example:

> But a stupid man will get understanding,
>   when a wild ass's colt is born a man.
> —11:12

In interpreting the book of Job one should remember the special features of Hebrew poetry.

Another literary consideration to keep in mind is the fact that Job is Wisdom Literature. Wisdom Literature was a special type of writing used in the ancient Near East. Egypt, Edom, and Mesopotamia have all yielded literature similar in some respects to the books of Job, Proverbs, and Ecclesiastes.[5]

Wisdom Literature in Israel was produced by a God-inspired religious leader, called a wise man. Such passages as Jeremiah 18:18 and Ezekiel 7:26 place the "counsel from the wise" on a par with the message of a priest or a prophet.

Wise men were concerned mainly with the practical art of living. For this reason they collected and taught universal truths expressed in short, pithy sayings which we call "proverbs." Such wise men produced the book of Proverbs and probably furnished much of the materials for Job and Ecclesiastes. Each of these books contains many "wise sayings."

However, among these wise men were some who were not satisfied with being collectors and teachers of proverbs. These restless spirits were concerned with the more basic problems and issues of life. Such men produced reflective and meditative works on the problem of the suffering of the righteous and the presence of injustice in the world.

Wisdom Literature can be identified on the basis of its theme, its vocabulary, and its use of proverbs. The book of Job qualifies as Wisdom Literature on all of these counts. It deals with some of the basic issues of life. Its vocabulary is crammed with words common to the wise man: fool, folly, wise, wisdom, understanding, and knowledge. The book of Job contains many examples of popular proverbs. (See 4:17; 5:7; 6:5; 7:9; 8:11; 11:7, 12; 12:11; 14:1, 14.) Chapter 28 is a great hymn in praise of wisdom. Any intelligent reading of the book of Job must take into account the fact that it is Wisdom Literature. However, though this book is classified as Wisdom Literature and has characteristics of the wisdom writings of its day, we are reminded that Job is uniquely inspired and is above the level of other wisdom literature of that time.

Wisdom Literature could take many forms. The question, then, is: What is the form of Job? Is it a drama? an epic? a tragedy such as Aeschylus' *Prometheus?* Is it history?

Job has been called a drama,[6] but if by drama we mean a production intended to be acted out on a stage, Job is not a drama. There is no action and very little plot in Job. The entire dramatic experience takes place with all the participants sitting on and around an ash heap, with no more activity than what is required to move their mouths.

Job is dramatic, but it is no drama. Some have called Job a tragedy. It certainly contains some tragic elements: the death of all of Job's children, the loss of his fortune, his great physical and mental anguish. But if we mean by a tragedy, "a serious play having an unhappy or disastrous ending brought about by the characters or hero impelled by fate or moral weakness, psychological maladjustment, or social pressures," Job is not a tragedy. Tragedy glorifies human resistance to God. Job glorifies human resistance to Satan and human subjection to God. Prometheus defied Zeus; Job laid his hand upon his mouth rather than curse God (40:4).

Job is not an epic. The book of Job shares elements with all of these literary types—wisdom literature, drama, tragedy, epic poem—but it cannot be classified as any one of them. It is best to say that the book of Job is itself!

The Historical Principle

The historical principle of interpretation tries to reconstruct the historical background of an ancient writing and determine the historicity of events, people, and places in it. What about the book of Job? When and where did Job live? Who wrote this book? Are the people, places, and events in the book historical? Such questions have been debated for centuries. It is impossible to answer with any degree of finality, for the biblical writer did not seek to answer these questions.

It was once popular to refer to Job as "the oldest book in the world." This assumption was based on its apparent patriarchal setting; its alleged silence concerning Mosaic laws and institutions; its failure to mention the major events in the history of Israel (Exodus, conquest, and the Davidic covenant); and its use of primitive names for God such as El and Shaddai.

The patriarchal setting of Job is generally acknowledged, but that does not require the book to have been written in patriarchal times. Job could have lived at one time, and the book could have been written at a later date. The silence of the book concerning the Mosaic laws and later events in the history of Israel does not prove either a Mosaic or a pre-Mosaic date for the book. There may be a better explanation of such silence.

Wisdom Literature is also silent about such matters as the tabernacle, Temple, priests, law, election, covenant, Jerusalem, the Messiah, and the latter days. Wisdom Literature makes no distinction between Israelites and Gentiles. In Job the characters seem to be Gentiles, but we are not told whether they are or not. Such matters are stronger indications that the book is Wisdom Literature than that it is "the oldest book in the world."

When was Job written? The Babylonian Talmud said that Moses wrote it. Martin Luther believed that Solomon was the author. Many of the more recent scholars have argued that the book in its present form could not be earlier than the time of Jeremiah. Job 3 and Jeremiah 20:14–18 are very similar. The problems of suffering and evil became very acute in the time of Jeremiah, due to the destruction of Jerusalem by Nebuchadnezzar. Habakkuk, who lived about the time of Jeremiah, began asking questions about evil and suffering and righteousness (Hab. 1:2–4, 13–17; 2:4). Some passages in Job seem to reflect a national calamity such as the fall of Jerusalem (see 9:24; 12:13–25; 24:12).

Job seems to have been written after Psalm 8, since there appears to be a parody of Psalm 8:4 in Job 7:17. The fact that Satan is mentioned in Job 1:6–12 and 2:1–7 may be evidence of a late date because the only other references to Satan (by this name) in the Old Testament are in Zechariah 3:1–2 and 1 Chronicles 21:1, both of which in date of writing are post-exilic. (In Psalm 109:6, KJV, the word "satan" seems to refer to a human adversary.)

Nothing is said in the book of Job about the identity of the author or authors. This lack of specific information has led to much speculation about authorship of the book. It is possible that more than one human hand and mind had a part in producing this work. Perhaps the story of the patriarch Job's sufferings became widespread and was handed down from generation to generation until a great poet, possibly sometime in the sixth century B.C., was inspired by the Spirit of God to write the book substantially as we have it now.

Some scholars regard the speeches of Elihu as a later addition. There also seems to be some confusion in the identity of the speakers in Job 25–27. We will discuss these problems when we come to the passages in our study. However, these problems, regardless of how one settles them in his own mind, do not negate inspiration of the Holy Spirit in the writing of this biblical material.

Is Job historical? It may come as a surprise or even a shock to some people to learn that as long ago as the early part of the Christian era some rabbis and some Christian leaders believed the book of Job to be a parable, meant to set forth different views about God's providence.

Martin Luther believed that the book of Job was history poetically idealized. In his *Table Talk* he said: "I hold the book to be real history: but that everything so happened and was so done I do not believe, but think that some ingenious, pious, and learned man composed it as it is."

John Calvin was a bit more literal than Luther in his views on Job. Calvin did not write a commentary on Job but he preached 159 sermons on the book. Calvin was not certain of when Job lived, but he was convinced that Job was a historical character and that the events recorded in the book took place as written.

Perhaps the best solution to the problem of the historicity of Job can still be expressed in the words of John R. Sampey:

> The Book of Job is neither literal history, nor purely the work of the imagination. We may accept the outlines of the story as historical, and yet accord to the great poet who wrote our present book large liberty in the handling of his material.[7]

The Theological Principle

The literary and historical principles, used properly, will tell us what the Bible says. But there is one further step to take in interpreting a passage; that is, what does the passage mean by what it says? In Scripture, the meaning is the main thing. It is possible to read the Bible historically and grammatically and miss the theological meaning. The theological principle of interpretation tries to determine the meaning, or message, of a passage or a book. But the theological meaning must take into account the grammatical and historical meaning.

Caution must be used in applying the theological principle. The spiritual truths of the Scriptures must be spiritually discerned (1 Cor. 2:13–14). However, the guidance which the Holy Spirit gives as we study is not the same as the inspiration he gave to the writers. We should never claim infallible guidance in understanding the Scripture. The Holy Spirit can influence our attitudes and perceptions. He does not give us information the Scriptures do not contain.

Two interpreters have pointed out that "the Spirit of God does not communicate to the mind of even a teachable, obedient, and devout Christian, any doctrine or meaning of Scripture which is not *contained already in Scripture itself.* He makes men wise *up* to what is written, not beyond it." [8] We cannot discuss here the meaning of each passage in Job. We will attempt to do that as we go through the book. However, we should consider briefly the overall meaning or purpose of the book.

The earliest view of the meaning of Job seems to have been that of showing the patience of a good man under testing. In the prologue Job is certainly pictured as an example of patience. This view is expressed in early Christian and Moslem literature. But Job is not very patient in the poetic sections of the book. To teach that a good man should be patient in suffering cannot be the only message or purpose of Job.

Some scholars have argued that the purpose of Job is to refute the prevalent doctrine that all suffering is due to sin, and all blessings—material, mental, emotional, and spiritual

—are the result of complete obedience to God. Such a doctrine was common throughout the Old Testament period. It was current in Jesus' day (Luke 13:1–3; John 9:1–3), and it is still with us.

The book of Job certainly does refute such a doctrine. It shows that a good man might suffer even as the wicked man. However, the poet does not deny that moral principles are operative in the world. There is room to believe that there is some connection between goodness and blessings and between sin and suffering, but the connection remains mysterious. Some people believe that the purpose of Job is to teach the mystery of suffering and to affirm that one should trust God, who alone knows the reasons why things are as they are.

Some scholars claim that Job was written to justify the ways of God with man; that it is a theodicy (a defense of God's goodness and power in view of the existence of God). They argue that the prologue justifies God's part in allowing Job to suffer as a means of meeting the challenge of Satan. Job's friends justify God's actions on their supposition that Job is suffering because of his sins. Elihu believes that God is disciplining Job. However, Job, the hero of the book, makes no attempt to justify God. And the speeches of Yahweh make no reference to the justice of God. The book of Job is not a theodicy.

Some writers have seen the purpose of the book in the implication of Satan that religion is basically selfish; that men serve God for what they can get out of him. Satan did assail all religions with his question, "Does Job fear [serve] God for nought?" (1:9). It is true that God often puts a hedge of protection and blessing around those who serve him. It is also true that sometimes he allows Satan to buffet severely the righteous man. Good people should be reminded by Job's experience that they have no right to expect favored treatment or reward because of their virtues. They have no right to charge God with wrong when they suffer. Justification comes only by faith and not by self-vindication.

One other suggestion as to the purpose of Job has merit; that is the suggestion that the book struggles with the problem of the remoteness and transcendence of God. *Job's real problem did not lie in the fact of his suffering; his real problem was in the fact that God was hidden from him.*

Lo, he passes by me, and I see him not;
he moves on, but I do not perceive him.
—9:11

Why dost thou hide thy face,
And count me as thy enemy?
—13:24

Oh, that I knew where I might find him,
that I might come even to his seat!
—23:3

Behold, I go forward, but he is not there;
and backward, but I cannot perceive him;
on the left hand I seek him, but I cannot behold him;
I turn to the right hand, but I cannot see him.
—23:8–9

Job's problem of the hiddenness of God is often our problem. How often do we call on God only to have the heavens seem to be brass? Job could not find God. He could not get a response from God, either yes or no. The feelings of abandonment, helplessness, and loneliness almost overwhelmed him. Such feelings are most acute when one is suffering from pain and loss. From his miserable place on the ash heap, Job felt that God had abandoned him. He was like the Jews in Babylon who said,

The Lord has forsaken me,
my Lord has forgotten me.
—Isaiah 49:14

Job's problem was that he was cut off from God. His problem was solved when God spoke to him out of the whirlwind.

Some interpreters have called the message of Job "existential." It speaks to the human situation. Job accepted life as it was and tried to understand what was happening to him. His world view was expanded when God spoke to him out of the whirlwind. God is so much greater than anything man can ever contemplate that it behooves man to place his hand on his mouth in the presence of God (40:4).

In praising the book of Job we must not overlook its limitations. Job was a B.C. man. He did not have all of the answers, because revelation was still incomplete. Also, the book of Job is limited in that the characters in the book are all wealthy, or at least are wealthy for a time. Can poor people, who have no fortune to lose, identify with Job? The book is limited in that the evils which confront Job are primarily physical and negative: loss of wealth, health, and children. Very little is said about the great moral and social evils with which we are concerned today, although some of those are mentioned in Job's oath of innocence (31:1–40). The book does not have a fully adequate view of sin. Several references in Job seem to teach that man is sinful simply because he is a man (4:17; 9:2; 15:14; 25:4–6). Compare Romans 3:23.

If the book of Job has an inadequate view of sin, it also has an inadequate view of salvation. Job was mainly concerned with salvation from suffering and isolation from God and man. Job's friends did admonish him to repent, and there is in the book recognition of a need of grace. There is no clear doctrine of atonement, and there is no full understanding of resurrection in the book. All of these doctrines—repentance, faith, grace, Messiah, and resurrection—are foreshadowed in Job, but they all had to wait many centuries before they were filled with complete meaning.

Job and the New Testament

There are very few direct quotations of the book of Job in the New Testament. It is not the kind of book that fits into the New Testament pattern, since it does not deal with the great redemptive acts of God. Some passages in Job may be reflected in some of the Gospels and in Paul's writings. Compare 1 Corinthians 1:24 with Job 12:16; 1 Corinthians 3:19 with Job 5:13; Romans 11:33 with Job 5:9; 11:7; Luke 1:52 with Job 5:11; 12:19; Matthew 19:26 and Mark 14:36 with Job 42:2; and Romans 2:19 with Job 29:15.

The most interesting relationship between the book of Job and the New Testament is at the point of innocent suffering. In the Old Testament animal sacrifices there was in a sense a case of the innocent suffering for another, but this was not a conscious or voluntary act. In Job we have an example of an innocent man suffering to demonstrate to angels and men that man can serve God, not primarily because of God's gifts but because of God himself. Paul may have had a similar idea in mind when he said: "I think that God hath set forth us the apostles last, as it were appointed to death: for we are made a spectacle unto the world, and to angels, and to men" (1 Cor. 4:9, KJV). The sufferings of Job were not voluntary. He was unaware of the real reason; he suffered almost against his own will because of his commitment to God.

There was another One who suffered because of his commitment to God. But unlike Job, he was sinless; and he suffered voluntarily not for himself but for the whole world. Suffering is not always evil. It can be redemptive. No doubt Job's suffering prepared him for hearing the voice of God in the whirlwind, and for interceding for his friends.

Conclusion

Some great truths stand out in any interpretation of Job: Virtue is not necessarily correlated with prosperity. Calamity is not certainly the result of misdeeds. Suffering may be an asset even to be coveted.

True repentance comes when one is brought face to face with the living God. God is just, sovereign, and always near, even when he seems to hide his face.

---

1. H. H. Rowley, *From Moses to Qumran* (New York: Association Press, 1963), p. 141.
2. For a survey of some of these versions see: Olin T. Binkley, *How to Study the Bible* (Nashville: Convention Press, 1969), pp. 16–21.
3. These two references in Job are two of eighteen places in the Old Testament which were changed. For a discussion of the other passages see: *Interpreter's Bible*, (Nashville: Abingdon Press, 1954), Vol. I, p. 51. The rabbis called such changes *Tiqqune Sopherim* "corrections of the scribes."
4. Ralph L. Smith, "Principles of Interpretation," *Encyclopedia of Southern Baptists*, ed. Norman W. Cox (Nashville: Broadman Press, 1958), Vol. I, pp. 689–690; Olin T. Binkley, *How to Study the Bible* (Nashville: Convention Press, 1969), pp. 37–48.
5. See my discussion of Wisdom Literature in: *Israel's Period of Progress* (Nashville: Convention Press, 1970), pp. 155–172.

6. See L. D. Johnson, *An Introduction to the Bible* (Nashville: Convention Press, 1969), p. 68.
7. John R. Sampey, *Syllabus for Old Testament Study* (Nashville: Broadman Press, 1924), p. 116.
8. Joseph Angus and Samuel G. Green, *The Cyclopedic Handbook to the Bible* (New York: Fleming H. Revell Co., 1908), p. 179.

2

From Riches to Ruin

(1:1 to 2:13)

Job, the Righteous Man (1:1–5)

The first paragraph of the book of Job furnishes a backdrop for everything else that happens in the book. It presents the Old Testament picture of a righteous man par excellence: a stalwart man properly related to God and to his fellows. Though Job was just such a man, he became one of the world's great sufferers. And there was absolutely nothing in Job's character or conduct to explain his suffering. Job's story has continued to raise the question, why should a righteous man suffer? But the answer to the question is not the major lesson to be learned from Job. Let us look first at the character of this man who endured such suffering.

A Real Man (1:1)

In the Old Testament a righteous man is a real flesh and blood man. The Hebrews did not think abstractly. For them, names, faces, and places were essential to telling stories and teaching truths. Thus the central character in the book of Job was not a nameless, faceless person but a man who lived in a particular place and had a personal name. It is true, we do not know exactly where the land of Uz was; but it was no fictitious place. The name Uz occurs eight times in the Old

Testament. In five instances it refers to a man. Three times Uz refers to a district or a land (Job 1:1; Jer. 25:20; Lam. 4:21).

There are at least two traditions concerning the location of the land of Uz mentioned in Job. One places it in Hauran, the region just east of the Sea of Galilee. Another puts it on the border of Edom. The Hauran tradition is supported by a statement from Josephus that Uz, son of Aram (Gen. 10:23), founded Trachonitis and Damascus; by the fact that Nahor, who lived in Haran (North Mesopotamia), had a son named Uz (Gen. 22:20, RSV); and by the fact that through the centuries there has been strong tradition that Job lived in that region. The tradition of Job is still alive today around the town of Nawa, twenty miles east of the Sea of Galilee, where ruins are still named for Job. Tourists are still shown tombs reputed to be that of Job and his wife, as well as a monastery, Deir Ayyub, which was named for Job.

While the evidence for the location of Uz in Hauran or Bashan is strong, most modern scholars prefer a location for Uz somewhere along the border of Edom. Job's friends were from Edom. Eliphaz was from Teman, one of the chief cities of Edom. It is impossible to determine the exact location of Uz, but such is not necessary to the understanding of the book.

Job not only lived in a particular place but he had a specific name. The name Job appears in Egyptian Execration Texts as early as 2000 B.C. One of the Amarna Letters, dating from about 1350 B.C., mentions a king of Ashtaroth in Bashan named *Ayyab* (Job). Many attempts have been made to find some symbolism or special meaning in the name Job. The history of the word is uncertain. Some think it means "enmity" or "hostility" referring either to Job's hostility or to him as the object of hostility. Some think it means "return" or "repent." Thus Job would be "the penitent one." With so little evidence, perhaps no special meaning should be assigned to Job's name.

A Whole Man (1:1)

A righteous man in the Old Testament was a whole man. Job's wholeness is described by four terms in verse 1: "blameless," "upright," "feared God," and "turned away from evil." (These terms are repeated in 1:8; 2:3.)

The first term "blameless" ("perfect," KJV), means to be whole, complete, healthy. It does not mean "sinless." The writer knew the importance of being whole because he was acquainted with people who were not whole but "hollow"—"stupid" (RSV) or "vain" (KJV). (See 11:12.) Job was not sinless, but he was honest. He possessed a basic and rugged integrity of character which showed itself in his dealings with God and man. He feared (reverenced) God and was upright in his dealings with his neighbors. The word "upright" means straight.

Job also avoided or "turned away from evil" (1:8; 2:3; 28:28). To turn away from evil means to reject resolutely opportunities to do evil (compare chap. 31). Job's personal integrity and proper social relationships were based on his religion (fear of God). Being a whole person psychologically and an adaptable person socially depends upon religion and morality.

A Family Man (1:2)

A righteous man in the Old Testament was a man of right family relationships. From the beginning the Bible puts its blessing on monogamy. Many wealthy and powerful men in the Old Testament had more than one wife, but the Bible never commends them for it. Job was a wealthy and powerful man (chap. 29), yet he had only one wife. He had an ideal family (seven sons and three daughters). Sons were considered rich blessings from God (Ps. 127:3–5). Therefore, we can conclude that Job's family was evidence of his righteousness.

A Rich Man (1:3)

A righteous man in the Old Testament, according to the Deuteronomic theology, was often a wealthy man. Job's wealth is described in terms of the typical seminomadic sheikh. His possessions are described in ideal figures and are probably listed in the order of their value: "seven thousand sheep, three thousand camels, five hundred yoke of oxen, five hundred she-asses, and very many servants" (1:3). (Nabal was a "very great man," yet he only had four thousand sheep and goats [1 Sam. 25:2]).

Nothing is said in this passage about any gold or land that Job might have owned. However, some indication of the amount of land Job controlled may be seen in the number of oxen he had. Oxen were used almost exclusively for cultivating the land. Since Job had five hundred yoke, his land holdings must have been immense. Eliphaz made reference to Job's possession of land in 22:8, and Job's gold is referred to in 22:24 and 31:24.

"And that man was the greatest of all the people [sons] of the East." Who are "the sons of the East"? Were they wise men (1 Kings 4:30) or natives of the region east of Israel or east of the Euphrates? Were they Israelites or foreigners? Many interpreters believe that these "sons of the east" were foreigners to Israel.

Whether Job was a foreigner or not is debatable. The phrase, "the greatest of all the sons of the East," probably means simply that Job was known and respected far and wide.

A Religious Man (1:4–5)

Job's affluence is seen in the fact that each of his sons had owned a house. The daughters probably lived with their father. The seven sons took turns in hosting a feast for the others and their sisters, "each on his day." A. B. Davidson suggested "his day" means the different days of the week. If so, life for Job's children was a continual round of festivals. Other scholars think that the reference is to the seven days of the annual New Year festival or the Feast of Tabernacles. Some have suggested "his day" refers to each son's birthday.

Perhaps the main emphasis in these verses is not on the affluence of Job's household or even upon how well the children got along together but upon Job's constant fear of God, (his awe, reverence, respect for God). He was mindful that temptation was always present and that his sons might sin or "curse God in their hearts." So, at the end of each festival

Job would send for his sons and offer a burnt offering for them. It is interesting that the sin of cursing God was the one which Job feared in his children; the one which Satan said Job would commit; and the one Job almost committed—not through the work of Satan but through the "comfort" of his friends!

This first paragraph (1:1–5) sets the stage for the trial of Job. Although he was the epitome of righteousness, his righteousness was going to be tested to see if it was real or a sham.

A Meeting of the Heavenly Council (1:6–12)

In the first two chapters of Job the scene shifts back and forth from earth to heaven like a metronome or a psychedelic flasher. The Hebrews, along with many of their Near Eastern neighbors, believed that the universe was made up of two worlds: the unseen world and the earthly world. The earthly world and its happenings were only reflections of what went on in the world above.

The Old Testament often pictures God on his throne, surrounded by angels who comprise his heavenly council and who carry out his decisions (see Isa. 6:1–3; 1 Kings 22:19–22). These heavenly beings were not to be worshiped. They had no decision-making power of their own. They could only do what God commanded or allowed them to do.

The decisions of the heavenly council were secret. Only the prophets were able to listen in on the secrets of the heavenly council. Amos 3:7 says, "Surely the Lord God does nothing without revealing his secret to his servants the prophets." A true prophet was one who had stood in the heavenly council and who became a messenger, or a spokesman, for God (see Isa. 6:1–6; Jer. 23:18, 22). But Job was not a prophet. He did not know what decision had been made in heaven concerning his fate. However, he did believe that whatever happened occurred not by mere chance or by accident but for some purpose, even though he might not know what that purpose was. H. L. Ellison wrote:

> For Job's contemporaries, as for the inhabitants of the Near East in general, and for Israel in particular for

> many centuries to come, a man's prosperity or adversity, his health or sickness, were regarded as the verdict of heaven on his conduct. Job himself believed this, and this belief lies in one form or another behind all the arguments of his friends.[1]

In his drawings on the book of Job, William Blake makes much use of this unseen world. Half of his drawings are two dimensional. They present on one level what was going on in heaven and on another level, what was going on in the world below. The book of Daniel speaks of a struggle going on in heaven between the various angels of the nations (Dan. 10: 13–21). The New Testament continues this Old Testament concept of heavenly powers both benevolent and antagonistic to man and his world (see Rom. 8:38; Eph. 6:11–12). Job was aware that greater than human forces were involved in his experience.

The Arrival of The Sons of God and the Satan (1:6)

The scene here appears to be that of the members of the heavenly council meeting periodically to report to God and to receive new orders.

Satan seems to have been a special participant in the heavenly council. The Hebrew word *satan* means adversary, or opponent. The angel of the Lord is called a "satan" in Numbers 22:22 when he opposed Balaam's going to Moab to curse Israel. Men were also called "satan" (see 1 Kings 5:4; Ps. 109:6). The commanders of the Philistines mentioned the possibility that David might become a "satan" (adversary) to them if he went with them to battle against Saul (1 Sam. 29:4). Hadad and Rezin are spoken of as "satans" (adversaries) to Solomon (1 Kings 11:14, 23,25).

Satan as a kind of spirit is mentioned only three times in the Old Testament (Job 1–2; Zech. 3:1–2; 1 Chron. 21:1). In all of these passages Satan is an accuser and an opponent of man, yet he is a strictly limited creature. The Hebrews believed in the sovereignty of God to control all power, including the power of evil.

Satan's Role (1:7)

In the book of Job, Satan seems to have had a wider mission than did the other members of the heavenly council. He was allowed to go throughout the whole earth seeking to discover the faults and infidelities of men and to report them to God. The word "Satan" always has the definite article in Job and Zechariah. Literally it is "the Satan." The article probably refers to "*the* adversary" of Job and, indirectly, of God. Here Satan's role is to test man's righteousness—to see if it is real or fake.

God's Confidence in Job (1:8)

Since God knew Satan's role, and since Job had been presented as a prime example of a righteous man, God challenged Satan to find some flaw in Job's righteousness. God called Job "my servant," which was a compliment to Job. Moses was called God's servant (Exod. 14:31), as was Caleb (Num. 14:24), David (2 Sam. 7:5, 8), Isaiah (Isa. 20:3), Zerubbabel (Hag. 2:23), the prophets (2 Kings 9:7), and the Suffering Servant (Isa. 52:13). Job is called God's servant four times in the epilogue. In verse 8, the words of verse 1 are repeated by God to validate Job's righteousness.

Satan's Indictment of Job and God (1:9–11)

Satan conceded that Job was righteous, but he brought an indictment against Job at the point of the genuineness of his righteousness. Job was righteous, but why was he righteous? Satan believed that Job had an ulterior motive for serving God. By his question, "Does Job fear God for nought?" Satan implied that Job was righteous only because of the rewards of his good life.

Many people still believe that man should be righteous so that God will bless them or because God will curse them if they are not righteous! The book of Job teaches that men should be righteous, not simply to gain peace of mind, health, wealth, or eternal life. It is true that many of these things are by-products of true righteousness and faith. However, they furnish no adequate ground for righteousness. Only God can provide that. God wants men to serve him because they love him and not the things he can give them.

If man, the only creature God made with a capacity to love, does not love God genuinely and of a free will, then God's purpose in creation has failed. Piety which depends on prosperity is not genuine. The only way to tell whether a man's piety depends on his prosperity is to remove his prosperity. That is what happened to Job. The harmony between goodness and well-being had to be broken in order to prove that Job's piety was solely for the sake of God.

Someone might ask, "Why all the bother?" Is not this a "cruel experiment" just to prove to Satan and the heavenly council that there is such a thing as basic human integrity and disinterested religion which is based on a love for God and not for rewards? One writer entitled her book on Job *The Cruel God.* But other scholars have defended the test of Job on the ground that an untested faith is an insufficient faith.

God was not trying to break Job's faith; he was trying to demonstrate it and validate it. God was honoring Job, since there is a sense in which Job was suffering for God, for himself (what he believed was right), and for others. Faith is constantly being tested. Job's was no isolated case. Perhaps his tests were more sudden and severe than most. But God has the right and the power to allow our faith to be tested, and he will. Satan and the world will certainly do all in their power to test our faith in order to break it. How many millions of readers have been blessed and strengthened by this book because Job's faith was tested and validated!

Job was not told that he was being tested. Had he been told, the experience would not have been a true test. To really discover what a man thinks of God, of himself, and of others, watch him while the pressure is on, while he is in the dark, and in trouble. But no charge of a cruel experiment should be made in Job's case. This was no idle exercise, no sham battle. Like the temptations of Jesus, the sufferings of Job were real. Job was suffering partly to vindicate God's creation and operation of the universe. God is prepared to show that his way is best, that it can and does produce integrity of character and faith, and that man can hold on to his faith in spite of afflictions which befall him.

In his indictment Satan pointed to the hedge of security which God had built around Job, his family, and all that he had (1:10). Satan believed that God was at least partly responsible for Job's selfishness. Job's security became the issue in the controversy. Satan objected to the hedge of security God placed around Job. Later, on the ash heap, Job objected because God had replaced the hedge of security with a hedge of confinement (3:23; 19:8; 23:17).

Satan said that God had increased (literally, "burst forth") Job's possessions. He asserted that if God were to touch all of Job's possessions and make them vanish, Job would curse God to his face, openly and publicly, so that everyone would know that Job was serving God only for his gifts.

God Allows Satan to Test Job (1:12)

Satan asked God to put his hand on Job. God refused, but he granted Satan permission to do anything he wished with Job's possessions. However, Satan was not to touch Job's person.

Job's Losses and Response (1:13–22)

Job's losses were phenomenal, complete, sudden, and inexplicable. The day started out like any other day. Perhaps Job had just finished offering a sacrifice for his children, as he had done for many years at the end of each cycle of feasts (1:5). Now they were to begin again at the home of the eldest son. "Then came a messenger to Job." (The Hebrew word for "messenger" is the same as "angel.") As far as Job knew, the servant who brought the message could have been like an angel bringing news of some good fortune. There is nothing in the text to indicate that Job had any inkling that the messenger was on a mission of sorrow.

How do you tell a person that he has suffered a great loss of property, health, or loved ones? How do you tell a person that he has a terminal illness? We try to tip people off ahead of time that bad news is on the way. We try to spare them the shock of a sudden announcement of misfortune. News reports of tragic accidents withhold the names of the victims until the next of kin have been informed privately. In the early days of our country, letters containing bad news were edged in black. But the news of Job's losses came in quick, successive reports with no attempt to soften the blows.

The Loss of Material Possessions (1:13–17)

The oxen were plowing (perhaps in the late fall) and the asses (used mainly for riding and carrying burdens) were grazing nearby. Suddenly the Sabeans (an Arab tribe probably from north Arabia) fell upon them, captured the animals, and killed the servants—except one who escaped to tell Job.

The agent of the destruction of the sheep was "the fire of God." The author did not elaborate on the nature of the fire. It might have been lightning or brimstone, as in the case of the destruction of Sodom and Gomorrah. It is idle to speculate on such matters. The point is that God allowed it (2:3). The agents of destruction in these four reports alternate between human and divine.

Job had three thousand camels, which represented a sizable fortune. They were captured by a roving band of Chaldeans, who divided themselves into three companies and by surprise overwhelmed and killed Job's servants.

The Loss of His Children (1:18–19)

The loss of a child for a true parent is always a heart-rending experience. Recall the words of David upon hearing the news of the death of Absalom: "O my son Absalom, my son, my son Absalom! Would I had died instead of you" (2 Sam. 18:33). When we remember that children were looked upon by the Hebrews as good gifts from God, and remember that Job lost not one son but seven along with three daughters, we are amazed at his stamina and his trust in God.

Job's Response: Mourning, Worship, and Praise (1:20–22)

In the prologue, Job is pictured as a very patient man. He did not cry out or lose control of himself. Calmly he arose (he had been sitting), rent his robe and shaved his head (performing the prescribed ritual of his faith appropriate in such a situation), fell to the ground and worshiped. Instead of cursing God as Satan said he would, Job worshiped God. He recognized that even the terrible things that had happened to him were not the result of blind fate but were the outworkings of divine Providence.

Job had been taught that his possessions were not his alone. They were gifts from God (1:21) which could be used as long as such seemed to suit God. Job knew that at death he would have to surrender his worldly goods, but the question now raised for him was: Does God have the right to take away all of a man's earthly goods before death? Job believed that God did. "The hand that has added without desert may subtract without reproach."[2]

Job found a proverbial saying adequate to express his reaction to his experience, "Naked I came from my mother's womb, and naked shall I return." The meaning is not that he will return to his mother's womb but probably is a reference to the womb of mother earth. Job said, "The Lord gave, and the Lord has taken away; blessed be the name of the Lord."

Job passed his first test. The author tells us, "In all this Job did not sin or charge God with wrong" (foolishness, or unworthiness). The meaning of the last phrase is that Job did not charge God with moral impropriety. Job recognized God's sovereignty and accepted that which had happened to him as a work of the mysterious providence of God.

In this age of advanced knowledge, can we still believe in the mysterious providence of God, or must we have a rational explanation of everything that happens and assign a cause to it? In Thornton Wilder's novel *The Bridge of San Luis Rey,* five people meet their death in the collapse of that bridge. A young priest, Brother Juniper, sets out to trace the lives of each victim to see if there was any order or purpose in their lives which might explain their seemingly untimely end. Amazingly, the priest found that in every case death came at exactly the right moment for each one of the victims. However, he himself was burned as a heretic for attempting to justify the ways of God to man. Job made no such effort; he accepted the ways of God in humble submission.

Another Heavenly Council Meeting (2:1–6)

In this section there is much repetition of terms used in the first council meeting. Three new elements appear. First, God called Satan's attention to Job's holding on to his integrity even though Satan "moved" God to destroy Job "without cause." Another new element is seen in Satan's proverb: "Skin for skin!" The meaning of the proverb is not quite clear. It could mean that Job was willing to trade other people's skin (that of his children and his servants) for his own. Or, it may be translated "skin after skin" as the *Anchor Bible* does.[3] Then it would mean that the first test of Job just covered the surface of the matter. Satan wanted to get to the heart of the testing, to get under Job's skin. The third thing that is new here is the limit set for Job's testing. Only Job's life was to be spared. Obviously, if the trial was to be a trial and not an execution, Job had to be kept alive.

Job's Loss of Health and the Temptation from His Wife (2:7–10)

Job's Affliction (2:7–8)

It would probably be a waste of time to try to determine the exact nature of Job's disease. Some interpreters have claimed that it was leprosy. Some have identified it with elephantiasis, a special kind of leprosy known in Egypt. Some see it as an especially severe case of skin infection or boils. One writer wisely commented that we are reading poetry, not pathology. Whatever it was that afflicted Job, it covered his entire body "from the sole of his foot to the crown of his head." And he took a potsherd (a broken piece of pottery) and scraped himself.

Job's Wife (2:9)

Job's wife has borne the brunt of much just or unjust criticism. She did advise her husband to do what Satan predicted he would do, curse God. She gave this advice knowing that death was the penalty for cursing God. Did Job's wife still believe in Job's righteousness? Or, had she fallen prey to the false doctrine that great suffering is the result of great sinning? It is probably best to believe that she still believed in her husband's righteousness but that she no longer could stand to see him suffer. Therefore, she advised him to take a theological method of committing suicide—to "curse God and die." The point of this incident probably was not to condemn Job's wife but to heighten the effect of Job's righteousness. Job was able to withstand such severe suffering that onlookers were overwhelmed by the fortitude he displayed through it all.

Job's Response (2:10)

Job rebuked his wife for her advice, but probably not too harshly. Muslim tradition says that Job struck his wife one blow with a palm branch having a hundred leaves.

Job stated his conclusion positively. "Shall we receive good at the hand of God and shall we not receive evil?" Can people who receive only good gifts from him believe in God? Can what seems to be evil also be intended as a good gift from God? Joseph said to his brothers: "As for you, you meant evil against me; but God meant it for good, to bring it about that many people should be kept alive" (Gen. 50:19–20).

"In all this Job did not sin with his lips." This statement does not suggest that he sinned in his heart. It only means that he did not sin as Satan said he would by cursing God publicly. Satan had lost his struggle. He had done all he could do to destroy Job's faith and righteousness. Job's suffering, as horrible as it was, did not blot out his memory of the grace of God. His *faith* remained steadfast. Satan does not appear again in the book, even though Job's trials were not over.

At this point in the book, a new episode in the drama of God's man is about to unfold. That episode involves Job's friends and Job's thoughts. What Satan could not do Job's friends almost accomplished.

The Visit of Job's Friends (2:11–13)

Job's three friends are represented in the Septuagint as kings. They were from Edom or Arabia. Jewish tradition says that they lived three hundred miles apart. We do not know how much time elapsed between Job's calamity and the arrival of his friends. But his suffering had taken such a toll on him that his friends did not recognize him when they first saw him. They observed the rituals of mourning and sat with him on the ground for seven days and seven nights (the period of mourning for the dead [Gen. 50:10; 1 Sam. 31:13]).

We should not be too critical of these friends. Someone has pointed out that three things can be said in their favor: (1) they came to visit Job when he was sick; (2) they remained silent a whole week in the presence of his great suffering; and (3) when they had something to say about Job they said it to his face and not behind his back. At least they had the courage of their convictions.

However, not everything about Job's three comforters is on the plus side. They failed in the very thing they attempted to do. They were miserable comforters and counselors. Today the role of counseling is a significant one. George Adam Smith said, "The speeches of Job's friends ought to be studied by every man who proposes to make the guidance and consolation of his fellow-men in their religious interests, the duty of his life."[4]

At first the friends were honest, sincere, and courteous. One interpreter has this to say, however:

> But the author shows how all the three comforters of Job misunderstood the heart; how little they have fathomed human experience; how easily worn out their love and patience; how they prefer to vindicate their own views of God to saving the soul of their brother; and how above all they commit the sin of not perceiving that God Himself may be working directly on that brother's heart, and purposes to teach them more than they can ever teach him. Love was what he looked for and trust: but they gave him argument which for a time only drove

him the further from God. You remember what he says:

> To him that is ready to faint kindness is due from his friend,
> Even to him that is forsaking the fear of the Almighty.
>
> —6:14

There is doubt about the true reading; but none can mistake the meaning. And yet how ignored this great verse has been! How different were the history of religion if men had kept it in mind! How much sweeter and swifter would the progress of Christianity have proved! The physicians of religious perplexity have too often been Job's comforters; and the souls in doubt, who should have been gathered to the heart of the Church with as much pity and care as the penitent or the mourner, have been scorned or cursed, or banished or even put to death.[5]

---

1. From *From Tragedy to Triumph* by H. L. Ellison; copyright © 1958 The Paternoster Press, Exeter, England. Used by permission.
2. Paul Sherer, *The Interpreter's Bible,* (Nashville: Abingdon Press, 1954), Vol. III, p. 917. This and all other quotes from *The Interpreter's Bible* used by permission of Abingdon Press.
3. Marvin Pope, *Job* "The Anchor Bible" (Garden City, New York: Doubleday and Company, 1965), pp. 18, 20–21.
4. George Adam Smith, *Modern Criticism and the Old Testament* (New York: A. C. Armstrong and Son, 1901), p. 298.
5. *Ibid.*, pp. 298–299.

3

Job's Soliloquy:
"Sick Unto Death"

(3:1–26)

CHAPTER 3 of Job is a pivotal chapter. It shows us how Job's mind changed as his pain intensified. In the prologue Job was patient, humble, reverent, faithful, and confident in God's providence. In this poetic section (chaps. 3–31) he is shown as impatient, proud, defiant, fearful, and in a state of doubt, despair, and protest much of the time. In the prologue Job was still suffering from the initial shock of disaster. In chapter 3 and beyond he pours out his own troubled thoughts of life and death and loneliness.

Chapter 3 is an outburst of pent-up emotion brought on by excruciating pain and anguish. It is one of the classic laments of the soul. We are told that Jonathan Swift, the gloomy satirist, on each evolving birthday, used to retire to his closet, shut the door behind him, and read this chapter. Many people in deep sorrow have found great spiritual consolation in Job's bitter words. It helps those in the valley of the shadow to know that others have walked that way before, and have come out into the light on the other side.

Chapter 3 deserves to be called a soliloquy (the act of talking to oneself), because it truly reflects Job's loneliness. He was not addressing God or his comforters. He was talking to himself, putting into words his innermost thoughts and feelings. The words are an indirect cry for help because Job already felt estranged from God and from his friends. (Compare 19:7; 24:12; 27:9; 30:24.) Great pain or sorrow often results in a break in communications between a man and his friends and sometimes between a man and his God.

We do not know how long Job waited quietly on the ash heap before his friends arrived. In 7:3 he spoke of being "allotted months of emptiness." Rabbi Aqiba assumed Job's affliction lasted a year. The "Testament of Job" reckons the time as seven years. After his friends arrived, Job remained silent seven days.

At the end of the seven days of mourning Job could endure the silence no longer. He was still human. He could not keep silent forever. He could not accept without a word of protest what seemed to him to be an unrighteous situation. So Job broke the silence with a curse against his birthday (3:1–10); then he asked why he did not die at birth (3:11–19); and finally he asked why he could not die at that moment (3:20–26).

Job Cursed His Birthday (3:1–10)

The phrase "after this" (3:1) joins the poetic third chapter of the prologue. Job sought to have the day of his birth and the night of his conception erased from the calendar (3:3). He desired that the day of his birth become black, dark, and gloomy, with no light in it at all (3:4–5). Then he expressed the desire that the night of his conception be eliminated from the calendar (3:6). He asked that that night be barren forever (3:7). Job knew stories of sea monsters (Leviathan) who were supposed to swallow the sun during an eclipse. He called for the night of his conception and the day of his birth to be swallowed up as Leviathan was supposed to have swallowed the sun (3:8–9, RSV). The reason for the curse on the night of his conception is given in verse 10. Since that night did not prevent his conception and birth, it was responsible for his seeing nothing but trouble.

A man who does not like birthdays is to be pitied. He has become disenchanted with life. Life itself has become a problem to him. One of the basic drives of man is the desire to live. The normal Israelite believed that life in any form is good. "He who is joined with all the living has hope, for a living dog is better than a dead lion" (Eccl. 9:4). When Job cursed the day of his birth, he was putting himself outside the normal thought patterns of Jews and Christians.

Job Asked Why He Did Not Die at Birth (3:11–19)

Job softened the curse of 3:1–10 to a question in verses 11–19. He asked why he did not die at birth. (Compare 10:18–19; Jer. 20:17.) The knees that received him (Job 3:12) may refer to his father's knees which recognized his legitimacy, or his mother's knees, or the knees of the midwife. Job thought that if he had died at birth, he would not only have escaped all of the sufferings he had endured but he would have enjoyed the "blessings" of death and Sheol. Job was a sick man, and a sick man's view of life and death is often far from normal. It has been said that the world of a sick man begins at his pillow and ends at the foot of his bed. The sick man is very shortsighted.

This passage (3:13–19) is one of the few in the Old Testament where death and Sheol (the grave) are presented as attractive. Here Sheol is pictured as a place of quietness, sleep, rest, and fellowship with the great and small of the earth. Prisoners are at ease, and slaves are free from toil. Other references in Job present death and Sheol in a different light. In 5:26 death is presented as the normal end of the long life of the righteous:

> You shall come to your grave in ripe old age,
>   as a shock of grain comes up the threshing floor in its season.
>
> —5:26

Death is the fate of all men (30:23), but sudden and premature death was viewed in early Israel as the result of wickedness (24:19; 34:20). Sheol, the place of the dead, is presented as a place of no return (7:10; 10:21; 16:22), of gloom and deep darkness (10:21), of uncleanness (9:31), rottenness (13:28), pain (14:22), fire (31:12), without wisdom (28:20–22), and a place that is open to the view of God (26:5–6).

Why Must a Wretched Man Live? (3:20–26)

In his wretchedness and bitterness, Job expressed a longing to die—an understandable but irresponsible feeling. Job may have been using a hyperbole here, because if indeed he had been about to die he might not have been so anxious to go. Job was in great pain physically (3:24, 26), and his mental and spiritual anguish was even greater. He asked:

> Why is light given to him who is in misery,
> and life to the bitter in soul?
>
> —3:20

> Why is light given to a man whose way is hid,
> whom God has hedged in?
>
> —3:23

God is mentioned for the first time in this chapter in verse 23. Job implied that God was responsible for all of his trouble. The hedge that had protected Job in his former estate (1:10) had now become a prison wall (3:23; compare 19:8; 23:17). The chapter ends on a note of poignancy and sadness:

> For my sighing comes as my bread,
> and my groanings are poured out like water.
> For the thing that I fear comes upon me,
> and what I dread befalls me.
> I am not at ease, nor am I quiet;
> I have no rest; but trouble comes.
>
> —3:24–26

Although Job's attitude toward life was very negative at this point in his religious pilgrimage, he did raise some issues that a modern man might have raised in the same situation. It should be stated, for instance, that Job, as far as we can tell, never contemplated suicide. Suicide is not an option for people who believe that God is the giver of life and the one to put an end to it.

Job did raise the ultimate questions of life and death. These questions are being asked among us today with a new intensity. What about euthanasia (mercy killing)? When is a man dead? Is it when his brain stops functioning or when his heart stops beating? The matter of birth raises for modern man further questions of artificial insemination, abortion, and the question of the population explosion. If the population is to be controlled, who is to say who will be born and who will not be born? To attempt to answer any or all of these questions would take us too far afield. But they present to us questions similar to the soul-searching ones which Job faced. What is life all about? Should the quality of life concern us?

Job's questions in chapter 3 show where he was in his religious pilgrimage. He was beginning to test the unquestioned tenets of his faith concerning righteousness and prosperity, sin and suffering, and the providences of God. But he had not forsaken God, and God had not forsaken him. Indeed, if God had forsaken Job it would truly have been better that he not have been born (compare Matt. 26:24).

Job's words in chapter 3 also furnish a beginning point for the replies of his three friends. They must have been shocked by Job's frankness, boldness, and pessimism. They probably interpreted Job's curse of his birthday and his statement about God hedging him in (3:23) as a charge against God. In his state of suffering, Job may have been more in touch with reality than were his friends.

4

The First Argument:

Is God Just?

(4:1 to 14:22)

HOW DOES ONE counsel a person who says that he hates life and longs to die? Job's words to that effect must have shocked his three friends as they sat silently beside him on his ash heap. They had traveled many miles at their own expense to be with him in his time of need, but they were not prepared for what they heard. They winced at Job's intemperate cry as he cursed the day of his birth (3:3–10), toyed with the idea of death (3:11–19), and challenged God's operation of the world (3:20–23).

The Three Friends

Because of their woefully inadequate theology of suffering, Job's friends were totally unprepared to cope with the situation before them. However, they could not remain silent. Such cursings, musings, and challenges had to be answered. So they plunged into a series of three arguments with Job. The first argument, or cycle of speeches, is recorded in chapters 4–14; the second in chapters 15–21; and the third in chapters 22–27.

Their Speeches

We call these cycles of speeches arguments rather than debates because they contain no formal debate terms such as "resolved" or "rebuttal." No major or minor premises are stated nor any proofs or deductions listed. There are only a few direct questions and answers on the part of the speakers. At times it seems that a speaker is so intent on getting his point across that he has not heard the previous speaker, or he completely ignores what the other person has said.

A basic courtesy is pictured in the arguments or dialogues. Each man is free to speak until he has finished. No one loses his turn (except Zophar, the third time around). There are no disruptions, riots, or any attempts to shout each other down. All of the speakers make much use of irony and sarcasm, which is not surprising under the circumstances.

It is very difficult to trace any real progress in the various speeches and cycles. It is true that the three friends became increasingly convinced of Job's guilt, but their theology never changed. Their tempers got shorter as their rhetoric got hotter.

Some progress may be detected in Job's thinking. He began in chapter 3 in a state of despair, asking to die. Prodded by the charges of guilt from his friends and conscious of his own integrity, he reflected on other possible solutions to his problems. He voiced a need for an umpire (9:33). He entertained the idea of a possible life after death (14:14). And he expressed the conviction that his Redeemer was alive and that he (Job) would eventually see God (19:25–27).

Job and his friends started out from the same theological vantage point. Much of what the friends said to Job is true. However, they did not leave room in their system for exceptions. They thought they had all truth, only to learn to their chagrin that they had applied their good theology in the wrong way. Job kept his theology close to life; they retained theirs in a creed.

We must not be too quick to condemn Job's friends. They were not coldhearted hypocrites. They were men of sincerity and integrity for whom suffering had not unlocked the door to God's larger world of mysterious grace. Another interpreter, Andrew Blackwood, Jr., wrote that Job's three friends were well-intentioned, thoughtful men who spoke too soon, said too much, and said the wrong things.

Characterization of the Friends

Many attempts have been made to describe the three friends of Job. Apparently Eliphaz was the oldest of the three. E. M. Good imagined that he had "a saintly face and white hair." H. L. Ellison said: "I always see him, not in the robes of an eastern gentleman, but in frock coat, striped trousers and top hat, the revered vicar's warden or senior deacon of a wealthy and fashionable church."

Bildad, who has been described as a retired army colonel, looked to tradition for his authority. All truth was once delivered to the fathers and closed tightly within a creed. Ellison says of Bildad:

> Left to himself he would probably have been a humble man, but he constituted himself a champion of the orthodoxy of the past. If he had lived at a later period, he would willingly have burnt Job's body in the hope of saving his soul . . . He has the rare gift of recognizing the first insidious inroads of false doctrine. . . . But . . . he is apt to be the church's worst friend in the hour of change and crisis. Above all, when men are sore tried and distressed, and the landmarks of life are hidden, it is seldom to Bildad that they turn.[1]

Zophar has been called "a man of the street," largely because of his harsh and uncouth language (11:6; 21:7, 12–18). T. H. Robinson accuses Zophar of being a dogmatic theologian "who speaks with 'authority' of his own certain knowledge, and needs neither justification nor support from any other source. He has no need to appeal either to direct experience of God or to wisdom of the past; he himself is wholly self-sufficient."[2]

The major difference between the three friends was not their theory of suffering or their attitude toward Job but their view of authority. Eliphaz appealed to his vision for his authority. He made his religious experience an infallible yardstick by which he measured the religion of others. H. L. Ellison noted that we have much to learn from Eliphaz: "A gospel without experience preached as the Gospel will repel all but those cut to our pattern."[3]

Zophar appealed to wisdom, his wisdom, for his authority. God's wisdom is beyond the reach of man, especially Job, but somehow Zophar felt that he spoke infallibly for God.

In the last analysis the three friends are just alike. They all believed that Job was guilty. Eliphaz manufactured a whole list of sins for Job (22:5–9). All three friends defended the retributive, or penal, view of suffering. All three were concerned more for the correctness of doctrine than for helping a brother through a mental, physical, and spiritual crisis.

The names of the three friends probably do not have any special significance. They are typical Near Eastern names. Some scholars suggest that Eliphaz probably means "God crushes." Bildad is short for "Darling of God." And Zophar may be translated in three ways: "Twittering Bird," "Jumping Goat," or "Sharp Nail."

There may be some questions concerning the feasibility of assigning a topic to the three cycles of speeches as I have done. Many themes are discussed in all three cycles of speeches, but the topics which I have listed are dominant themes in each of the three cycles. *The major theme of the first cycle or argument (4:1 to 14:22) is "Is God just?" The second cycle or argument (15:1 to 21:34) or major theme is "the fate of the wicked." The theme of the third cycle or argument (22:1 to 27:23) is "the sinfulness of Job."*

Eliphaz—The Voice of Experience (4:1 to 5:27)

Eliphaz' Opening Lines (4:1–11)

The beginning of a sermon, novel, play, or any piece of literature is important. Every writer or speaker wants to capture the attention of his readers or hearers at the very first. Eliphaz began his first speech to Job quietly and almost apologetically. "If one ventures a word with you, will you be offended?" Then he confessed that he had to speak whether Job was offended or not. He was like Elihu, who later said that he was "full of words, . . . his heart was like wine that has no vent, and wineskins ready to burst" (32:18–19).

Eliphaz expressed his surprise that Job could not take misfortune well. Job had often comforted others in their misfortunes (4:3–5; compare 29:12–16), but now suffering had come to him, and he was very impatient. Eliphaz mentioned two pillars of strength (4:6) which should have supported Job in his hour of crisis, and they did. Those two pillars were Job's fear of God and his integrity (see 28:28). Job never gave up these sources of confidence and hope.

In 4:7–11 Eliphaz set out his theology of punishment. Simply stated it is this: The righteous man will be blessed, and the wicked man will be cursed. Job 4:8 reminds us of Paul's statement in Galatians 6:7, "Whatsoever a man soweth that shall he also reap" (KJV). This statement is true, as is Eliphaz' statement, "Those who plow iniquity and sow trouble reap the same." However, the reverse is not always true. Some people reap trouble who do not sow iniquity, and that was Job's problem.

Notice that Eliphaz based his assertion on his experiences: "As I have seen. . ." (4:8). "I have seen the fool. . ." (5:3). "Lo, this we have searched out, it is true" (5:27). And in a later speech: "I will show you, hear me; and what I have seen I will declare" (15:17). Experiences are important, but they are not always reliable guides to the nature of reality.

It is interesting to observe in passing that there are five different words for "lion" in 4:10–11. In these verses the elimination of the wicked is compared to the destruction of a den of lions. Lions may roar, but when the hunter moves in, it is all over.

Eliphaz' "Religious Experience" (4:12 to 5:7)

Eliphaz did not depend on his physical senses alone for knowledge. He related an experience of a vision or a dream which greatly colored his theology (4:12–16). This was a rather eerie and spooky experience for Eliphaz, one which made his hair stand on end. Eliphaz did not see God or even a form to represent God. God is far too transcendent to be seen of men (John 1:18). But Eliphaz heard a voice say:

> Can mortal man be righteous before God?
> Can a man be pure before his Maker?
> Even in his servants he puts no trust,

And his angels he charges with error;
how much more those who dwell in houses of clay,
whose foundation is in the dust,
who are crushed before the moth.
Between morning and evening they are destroyed;
they perish for ever without any regarding it.
If their tent-cord is plucked up within them,
do they not die, and that without wisdom?
—4:17–21

We might have expected more from a vision that took five verses to introduce (4:12–16). The voice in Eliphaz' vision spoke very little that was new, and nothing that helped to comfort Job. No one was questioning the fact that God is greater than man (4:17). However, Eliphaz seemed to deduce from his doctrine of the greatness of God that all of creation, including the angels and men (4:18–19), are sinful and that man's life is very short, comparable to only one day. According to this friend, man dies suddenly and nobody cares (4:20). He does not live long enough to attain wisdom (4:21). In trying to defend God against Job's charge of injustice, Eliphaz argued that only God is pure, and all men are sinners.

Eliphaz speaks as if he were a deist who believes that God has abandoned his world. He makes God so transcendent (far above and surpassing man, "unlimitedness") that he robs the Almighty of all passion. Eliphaz believed that man is cursed as a moth, "without any regarding it" (4:20). Man lives in a house of clay (v. 19) whose foundation is dust. (Compare Gen. 2:7; 3:19; 2 Cor. 4:7; 5:1.)

In 5:1 Eliphaz continued his thought of the transcendence of God, the God who is so remote that he cannot be addressed directly. Job must, according to Eliphaz, use intermediaries. But if Job thought that he could get a "holy one" (angel) to intercede for him, he is mistaken; because angels know that no man can be righteous before God.

Eliphaz said that only fools resent God's dealings with them, and such "vexation" leads to their early demise (5:2). Eliphaz gave an example of a foolish man he knew who prospered for a time, then his dwelling was cursed. The expression of Eliphaz, "I cursed" (5:3) probably means, "I recognized as being cursed." Eliphaz seems to have been saying that the foolish man who complains about God's dealings with him perishes along with his family and property (5:4–5).

What is the source of evil? Chapter 5:6–7 seems to be saying that evil or trouble is not naturally a part of the world, but man is responsible for his own trouble. He brings sorrow on himself by his sinful ways. This idea seems to be different from the view Eliphaz expressed in 4:17–19 that man is a sinner simply because he is a man. There Eliphaz made man's human limitations equivalent with sin. That is, man does not have to do anything to be sinful; and, therefore, he is subject to suffering whether or not he commits any overt act of sin. Here he holds the view of retribution: suffering is the result of man's sins.

Advises Job to Seek God (5:8–16)

In this passage we get a little better look at Eliphaz' view of God. Eliphaz does not appear as a deist here. God's sovereignty is stressed rather than his transcendence. Here we see a God who is always doing things too great and too numerous for man to comprehend. (Compare 9:10; Rom. 11:33.) He sends the rain; he exalts the lowly and protects those who mourn; he frustrates the crafty; and he saves the fatherless, the needy, and the poor. This passage is surely defense of the justice of God.

It is interesting to observe that Job acknowledged God's great and mysterious power, as did the friends. But where the friends stressed the kindness and creative function of God's power, Job emphasized the negative and destructive manifestation of it (9:5–10; 12:7–25). The first line of 5:13 is the only direct quotation of Job in the New Testament (1 Cor. 3:19).

Believes that God Is Only Chastening Job (5:17–27)

Eliphaz seems to have modified his view of retributive suffering in Job's case. He did not believe that Job's suffering was fatal, but that God had brought trouble upon him to get him to repent. The view that suffering may be disciplinary is rather common in the Old Testament. Eliphaz said:

> Behold, happy is the man whom God reproves;
> therefore despise not the chastening of the Almighty.
> —5:17

Elihu (who came on the scene much later) was the main advocate of the disciplinary view of suffering. He said:

> Man is also chastened with pain upon his bed,
> and with continual strife in his bones.
> —33:19

> Then man prays to God, and he accepts him,
> he comes into his presence with joy.
> —33:26

> Behold, God does all these things,
> twice, three times, with a man,
> to bring back his soul from the Pit,
> that he may see the light of life.
> —33:29–30

> He delivers the afflicted by their affliction,
> and opens their ear by adversity.
> —36:15

The classical statement of the disciplinary view of suffering in the Old Testament is, perhaps, in Proverbs 3:11–12:

> My son, do not despise the Lord's discipline
> or be weary of his reproof,
> for the Lord reproves him whom he loves,
> as a father the son in whom he delights.

The disciplinary view of Job's suffering fits this stage of Eliphaz' thought. He was convinced that Job would be restored to his former estate and to a bright future (5:18–27).

Job's Response to Eliphaz and Prayer to God (6:1 to 7:21)

Job Defends His Vexation (6:1–7)

Eliphaz had stung Job with his words in 5:2, "Surely vexation kills the fool." Job did not appreciate being called a fool; he felt that he had just cause for his vexation because of the way God had treated him. He said that if his vexation, or his calamity which gave rise to his vexation, were weighed it would be heavier than the sand of the sea. Therefore, he felt, he was justified in speaking as he did in chapter 3. He said that God had been shooting him with poisoned arrows (6:4). Then he used two proverbs to express the naturalness of his protest (6:5) and the tastelessness of either Eliphaz' counsel or his own repulsive situation (6:6–7).

Job Repeats His Request to Die (6:8–13)

Here Job reverted to the thoughts he expressed in his soliloquy. He repeated his request to die (6:8). He had no intention of taking his own life, because he recognized that only God has the right to take life. But he prayed that God would let loose his hand and cut him off (6:9), because his pain was unsparing and he was innocent (6:10). Job had reached the end of his own strength. Evidently he did not know what another wise man discovered, that when a man exhausts his own strength God has resources available for him. The psalmist said:

> My flesh and my heart may fail,
> but God is the strength of my heart and my portion for ever.
> —Psalm 73:26

But at this point in his suffering, Job did not share this psalmist's faith nor Eliphaz' glowing promises.

Job's Friends Failed (6:14–30)

Job 6:14 illustrates some of the difficulties in translating parts of Job. This verse is difficult because the first Hebrew word in the verse occurs only here and because the conjunction at the beginning of the second line can be read "and," "but," "even." The ancient versions (Syriac and Vulgate) do not agree with the existing Hebrew text. The verse has been read many different ways. Moffatt and Delitzsch understand the verse to say that a friend (or friends) should show kindness to a despairing man *to keep him from losing his religion* ("fear of the Almighty").

Friends should be kind to a despairing man,
or he will give up faith in the Almighty.
—Moffatt[4]

To him who is consumed gentleness is due from his friend
Otherwise he might forsake the fear of the Almighty.
—Delitzsch[5]

The American Standard Version, Smith and Goodspeed, the New English Bible, and the Anchor Bible understand the verse to say that a friend should show kindness to a sufferer even though the sufferer has given up his faith in God.

To him that is ready to faint kindness *should be showed from a friend;*
Even to him that forsaketh the fear of the Almighty.
—Job 6 : 14, ASV

To him who is dissolving there should be kindness from his friend,
Though he forsake the fear of the Almighty.
—Job 6 : 14, Goodspeed[6]

Devotion is due from his friends
to one who despairs and loses faith in the Almighty.
—Job 6 : 14, NEB[7]

A sick man should have the loyalty of his friend,
Even if he renounce fear of Shaddai[8]
—Job 6 : 14, The Anchor Bible

The Revised Standard Version adopts the reading of the Syriac, Vulgate, and possibly the Talmud, following S. R. Driver and others, and understands the verse in a totally different light. The Revised Standard Version reads,

He who withholds kindness from a friend
forsakes the fear of the Almighty.
—Job 6 : 14

This last translation is the boldest, and, although it does not have the support of the standard Hebrew text, it appeals to the modern mind. It says that *failure to show kindness to a friend nullifies all of man's claims to be religious.* This sounds much like Amos and other Old Testament prophets. This interpretation underscores the fact that failure to do acts of kindness is irreligious, too.

The second type of translation (that represented by ASV, Smith-Goodspeed, and others) is modern also. It says that a sufferer's loss of faith should not be grounds for disrupting friendship. We now know from clinical studies that a person's physical illness can produce mental and spiritual problems. Such a person needs a friend then more than at other times. This is likely what Job was saying to his friends. He charged them with being fair-weather friends. When they thought he had given up his faith, they stopped being his friends. (Think of the relevance of this charge for our outreach actions!)

Job used two metaphors to illustrate their deceitfulness in pretending to be friends when in reality they were not. In 6:15–16 he accused them of being like a wadi (usually dry bed of a desert stream) filled with cold, icy water in the spring. But in the summer, when water is needed, these gullies are like dry river beds. In 6:17–20 Job compared his friends to an oasis that dries up in hot weather. Job accused his friends of being afraid of him, probably because they did not want to be contaminated by him (6:21). Job said that he had not asked them for anything. They should still be his friends.

H. L. Ellison has said,

> All Job had asked of his friends was understanding and sympathy, not money (6:22) or valiant deeds (6:23). Ironically enough, but entirely consistent with human nature, he would probably have received the latter had he asked for them. True sympathy and understanding are always costlier than charity.[9]

In 6:24–30 Job said that his friends had failed to prove one instance in which he had erred. He believed them to be heartless:

> You would even cast lots over the fatherless,
> and bargain over your friend.
>
> —6:27

Job suggested (6:28–29) that his friends had turned from him, unable either to look upon his condition or to listen to his rantings. Their reproof was empty and they lacked basic human sympathy.

Had Job's God Failed? (7:1–21)

From the failure of his friends, Job turned to his plight and, without actually putting it in words, indicted God's governing of the universe, especially God's dealing with men. Job complained in 7:1–2 that life for mankind as a whole is the miserable lot of a slave or a hireling who longs for the shadow or for payday. He said that he had no choice about his birth or his niche in life: "I am allotted [literally, "I inherited"] months of emptiness, and nights of misery are measured out to me" (7:3). A good example of a paradox is seen in 7:4 and 6. In one verse Job complained that his sleepless nights were too long; in the other he bemoaned the fact that his days were so short and were all spent without hope.

From his friends he turned to God and prayed for relief and release (7:7–21). All of Job's speeches show this turning from men to God. This is significant since Job regarded God as the author of his distress. There are really two dialogues going at once in this section of Job: one between Job and his friends and the other between Job and God. However, it would not be quite accurate to call the second a dialogue, since God remained silent in this section of the book.

Job prayed that God would remember that his life was like a breath (7:7) and a cloud that fades and vanishes (7:9). Therefore, Job decided to say what he had to say while there was time (7:11; compare 10:1). He asked why God was spying on him all the time as if he were some giant sea monster (7:12–19). He asked why God made such a "to do" over him. In his parody of Psalm 8:4, Job inquired of God why it was that he would bother with such an insignificant insect as man.

Marvin Pope said about this passage, "What in happier circumstances would be regarded as providential care is here ironically presented as overbearing inquisitiveness and unrelenting surveillance." [10] James Wood wrote that "Job sees God's interest in man, not as a loving concern, but as the watchful eye of a spy. God is not the loving Father in Heaven. He is the Big Brother of the police state." [11] H. G. Wells tells of a great eye painted on one of the walls of his Sunday School rooms when he was a boy. The inscription underneath was "Thou God seest me" (Gen. 16:13).

Job's accusation that God was spying on him may have been a betrayal of a guilty conscience. Job was not admitting that he had sinned; but he suggested that if he had sinned, his sin would not affect God (7:20). Job, like Eliphaz, was thinking of God as too high to be concerned with man or with anything he does (see 22:2–3).

Job used the word "sin" for the first time in 7:20. He had an inadequate view of sin in that he seems to have thought that sin has nothing to do with God. In 7:21 Job used the other two main Hebrew words for sin: "transgression" and "iniquity." He asked why God did not pardon his transgression and take away his iniquity. Voltaire once said, "God will forgive me, it's his job."

At this stage, Job did not know that sin is essentially rebellion against God; that sin does affect God; and that God does not forgive sins automatically. Ironically, Job betrayed in this passage the thought that God still cared for him. Job questioned God: "Why have I become a burden to thee?" (7:20). And in 7:21 he said, "Thou wilt seek me, but I shall not be." At the end of his debate with Eliphaz, Job was a bewildered and lonely man—his problem more acute than it was before the debate began.

Bildad—The Voice of Tradition (8:1–22)

Quick Rebuke of Job (8:1–2)

Bildad began with an emotional reaction to Job's complaints. If Bildad did not begin the practice of name-calling and the use of labels, he certainly engaged in such activity. He called Job a windbag. "The words of your mouth [are] a great wind" (v. 2).

Defends God's Justice (8:3–10)

Bildad was a man on the defensive. He believed that Job had attacked the doctrine of the justice of God, and he jumped to God's defense (8:3). Pitilessly he used the example of the loss of Job's children to defend his (Bildad's) theology of retribution. He asserted that Job's children sinned, and God delivered them into the power of their transgression. For Bildad, this was the only possible explanation. His theology dictated his conclusions. God could not be unjust; therefore, Job's children must have sinned. Bildad never imagined that there could be some other factor involved or some other explanation of Job's suffering. Evidently he was not aware that there is a vast amount of unmerited suffering in the world. Bildad certainly would have made a poor pastoral counselor in this complex age!

Piously, Bildad told Job that he should seek God and pray (8:5); and, if Job was pure and upright, God would reward him so that his latter days would be greater than his former ones (8:6–7). That is perilously close to the theology of Satan. Such a theology can be basically selfish and promote a religion of works rather than one of grace and faith. Bildad's theology was simple, shallow, and wooden. It was based on tradition. He said:

> For inquire, I pray you, of bygone ages,
>   and consider what the fathers have found;
> for we are but of yesterday, and know nothing,
>   for our days on earth are a shadow.
> Will they not teach you, and tell you,
>   and utter words out of their understanding?
>
> —8:8–10

There is nothing wrong with tradition as long as it is not canonized, credalized, fossilized, and deified. People need to be aware of their past in order to profit by the mistakes and the successes of their fathers. But situations change. New problems and opportunities arise. Yesterday's answers or methods may not be sufficient for today's problems and opportunities. In the folk musical, "Tell It Like It Is," the younger generation admonish their parents, "Don't tell us about the good old days, the days that might have been." The young people go on to say that their parents may have had the answers to yesterday's problems down pat, but today's youth have new problems which, in many cases, do not fit the old answers.

In fact, giving pat answers to contemporary questions seems to have been Bildad's problem. He had some very good answers, but they did not fit Job's situation because he did not understand Job's problem. We must admire Bildad for his confidence in the justice of God, for his willingness to stand up for his faith, and for his loyalty to the traditions of his fathers. But we must deplore his easy answers, his complicated questions, and his appeal to tradition to stifle even honest doubt and to foil every change. And we must avoid the mistakes of Bildad in our effort to counsel others.

James A. Froude has said:

> Periods of religious transitions, therefore, when the advance has been a real one, always have been violent, and probably will always continue to be so. They to whom the precious gift of fresh light has been given are called upon to exhibit their credentials as teachers in suffering for it. They, and those who oppose them, have alike a sacred cause: and the fearful spectacle arises of earnest, vehement men, contending against each other as for their own souls, in fiery struggle. Persecution comes, and martyrdoms and religious wars; and at last, the old faith, like the phoenix, expires upon its altar, and the new arises out of its ashes.[12]

H. L. Ellison contrasts Bildad's enslavement to the past with the view of John Robinson in his address to the Pilgrims at Delfshaven in 1620, just before they left for the New World:

> I charge you before God and His blessed angels, that you follow me no farther than you have seen me follow the Lord Jesus Christ. If God reveals anything to you by any other instruments of His, be as ready to receive it as you were to receive any truth by my ministry, for I am verily persuaded the Lord hath more truth to break forth out of His holy Word. For my part, I cannot suffi-

> ciently bewail the condition of those reformed churches which are come to a period in religion, and will go, at present, no farther than the instruments of their reformation.[13]

Bildad would go no farther than the tradition of his fathers took him. For him, all truth was delivered once for all in the past; moderns knew nothing. "For we are but of yesterday and know nothing" (8:9).

God Will Destroy the Wicked and Uphold the Righteous, Including Job (8:11–22)

With the use of proverbs and metaphors taken from the traditions of the fathers, Bildad pictured the fate of the godless man. He will perish as surely as a reed will die out of water (8:11). His confidence is as flimsy as a spider's web (8:14). He leans against his house, and it collapses. The godless are like plants which spring up in thin or rocky soil, thrive briefly, then wither, die, and are forgotten (8:16–18). The reference to "joy" in 8:19 must be irony.

Bildad concluded with the affirmation that God will not cast off a blameless man (8:20–22). The word "blameless" was used of Job in the prologue. Bildad was saying that if Job was blameless he had nothing to fear. This word "blameless" is the key to Job's reply to his would-be comforter Bildad (see 9:20–22).

Job's Reply to Bildad and Eliphaz and His Prayer (9:1 to 10:22)

Job Agrees Quickly with His Friends (9:1–2)

When Job said, "Truly I know that it is so," we do not know whether he was agreeing with Bildad or Eliphaz or both. Later (9:20, 22, 24) Job seems to have challenged Bildad's statement that "God will not reject a blameless man, nor take the hand of evildoers" (8:20). Therefore, we may assume that Job was agreeing with Eliphaz in 9:2 rather than with Bildad. Job 9:2–10 seems to indicate that there was a delayed reaction to Eliphaz' speech recorded in chapters 4 and 5.

Job Asks How a Man Can Be Just Before God (9:2b–10)

Eliphaz asked this question in 4:17 and concluded that man could not be just before God because of the sinfulness of man. Job believed that man cannot be just before God because God is arbitrary and all-powerful. He said that it is impossible for a man to contend with God (9:3). This is very bold language. It took a very brave man even to conceive of hauling God into court and putting him on trial. This is legal language and covenant language.

The Hebrew word *rîb* (contend) is a common word in the prophets (Isa. 3:13; Jer. 2:9; Hos. 4:1; 12:3; Mic. 6:2), but in those references it is always God contending with Israel. Here Job was contending with God. It is true that Abraham interceded (or contended) with God at length for Sodom, and Moses argued with God about going back to Egypt to bring the Hebrews out. Moses also boldly implored God to turn away from his wrath against Israel "and repent of this evil against thy people" (Exod. 32:11–12). Jonah argued with God about the advisability of preaching to Nineveh.

But Job was the boldest of all the confronters of God. He wanted to put God on the witness stand (compare 13:22), but he knew that such is impossible. Man cannot subject God to an inquisition, else God would be the creature and not the Creator. If man were to face God in court, man could not answer one out of a thousand questions God might ask him (9:3). Job was impressed with the negative and destructive aspects of the acts of God (9:5–8). God moves mountains and shakes the earth out of its place. He commands the sun and it does not rise; he seals up the stars so that they no longer shine.

Job recognized the gulf between God and man (9:32), but it is not just the gulf between the finite and the infinite. Job seems to have felt that there is something sinister about God. He is always causing earthquakes, darkness, sorrow, and woes. Here Job was thinking out loud. A man does not always mean everything he says when he says everything he thinks. But this was the way Job felt and the way countless numbers of his fellow sufferers feel. At this point, Job does not seem to have been very patient. But when one remembers that he was covered with boils, bereft of his children, tormented by his religious friends, yet was honestly seeking a satisfactory answer to his human situation, we can sympathize with him.

The rabbis said, "A man may not be held responsible for what he does in anguish." Job was asking questions of God and expressing doubts about God's justice. There is nothing inherently evil about doubting. It has been well said that one way to avoid facing doubts is to refuse to think. Job had the courage to think, whereas his friends merely echoed platitudes. And Job was the one God chose.

Again, Job said that it is impossible for a man to be just before God because man cannot find God. For Job, God was a hidden God (9:11; 13:24; 19:7; 23:3, 8, 9). Job said that God is autonomous. He does whatever he pleases, and none can stop him:

> Behold, he snatches away; who can hinder him?
>   Who will say to him, "What doest thou"?
> God will not turn back his anger;
>   beneath him bowed the helpers of Rahab.
>
> —9:12–13

In 9:14 Job began again to think of arguing his case in court and asserting his innocence before God, but now Job had become skeptical. He said:

> If I summoned him and he answered me,
>   I would not believe that he was listening to my voice.
> For he curses me with a tempest,
>   and multiplies my wounds without cause."
>
> —9:16–17

Job maintained that it would be impossible to get a fair trial before God, for even though he were innocent God would condemn him, and though he were blameless God would count him perverse (9:20). Job said that God destroys both the blameless and the wicked. When disaster comes, he mocks at the calamity of the innocent (9:22–23). The tormented believed that there is no justice in the world. And he asked, if God is not to blame for all this, who is? (See 9:24.)

Are Job's assertions true? Does God laugh at the calamity of the innocent? Has he given the earth into the hand of the wicked? To a person who had suffered as Job suffered and who had grown up with a theology strong on the sovereignty of God, it might seem so. A soldier in World War I was mortally wounded one hour before the armistice was reached. When the whistles began to blow and the bells began to ring announcing the end of the war, the dying soldier looked up into the face of the chaplain and said, "Isn't that just like God?" But is that like God? Was God responsible for any man being killed in the war?

Harry Emerson Fosdick [14] suggested four things which contain the source of our misery: "the law-abiding nature of the universe and the operation of natural law; human ignorance and the progressive nature of human life; the operation of man's freedom to choose; the togetherness and interdependence of human beings."

Fosdick's reasons do not deal with the theological problem of God's goodness in relationship to his omnipotence. John Stuart Mill gave this problem its classical shape when he asked, "How can there be suffering in a world created by a good omnipotent God?" Mill reasoned that if God is good, then suffering in the world must happen because God cannot help it. If that is the case, he is not all-powerful. On the other hand, if God is all-powerful and does not prevent suffering or speedily end it, how can he be good? The logical conclusion, according to this reasoning, is that God cannot be at one time all-powerful and good.[15] This, essentially, was Job's problem, although Job reached this point, not through logic, as did John Stuart Mill, but through bitter experience. While Job raised serious questions about the goodness of God, he had no doubts about God's omnipotence. However, this is not the last word of Job on the subject. We must look further.

Job's Present Plight (9:25–35)

Job turned for a moment from his charge against God to the plight he was in. This time it was not his suffering that impressed him but the swiftness with which his life was speeding to a close. Job used three metaphors to describe how his life was flying by. He said,

> My days are swifter than a runner;
>   they flee away, they see no good.
> They go by like skiffs of reed,
>   Like an eagle swooping on the prey
>
> —9:25–26

In 9:27 Job declared that he could not pretend to be happy when he was not. How many people try to wear a cheerful countenance when their heart is about to break? Job said that he could not do that because he knew that God would not hold him innocent (9:28).

Job was about ready to give up the struggle when he said:

> I shall be condemned;
>   why then do I labor in vain?
> If I wash myself with snow,
>   and cleanse my hands with lye,
> yet thou wilt plunge me into a pit,
>   and my own clothes will abhor me.
>
> —9:29–31

Job asked, "What is the use of striving to be innocent if it is impossible to justify oneself before God?" Ah, but there's the rub. Man cannot justify himself! Here is one of the momentous truths of the Bible, and one which twentieth-century man has forgotten: Man, spiritually speaking, is in the ditch and cannot get out by himself. Thus, Job was led to think that if God would not justify man but kept pushing him into the ditch (9:31), and if man cannot cleanse himself (9:30), perhaps there could be an umpire (9:33) who might lay his hand on Job and God and bring them together. What a thought!

We should be careful not to read too much into Job's understanding at this point. He probably had not followed his thought to its logical conclusion either in terms of ultimate justice or in the direction of the incarnation of the New Testament. But he was on his way. Job was not asking for an imposed settlement of his difficulties with God. He had a deep longing for one who could place his hand on God and on man and bring them together. He was asking for an arbiter, a go-between. Such a person would have to have the confidence of both: one who could represent man to God in man's alienation, and one who could mediate God to man in God's seeming aloofness.

Job sought understanding, love, and reconciliation, and he recognized the theological impasse of his human situation. Job's was not prophetic insight, at least not consciously, but his cry to God for a mediator can find its greatest meaning in the New Testament, in the incarnation. For a moment he toyed with the idea which ultimately was revealed as God's solution to this problem—the incarnation. Then Job dropped back again in his plight of the moment. In 9:34–35 he asked that God might get off of his back, then he (Job) would try to speak to God again without an umpire.

Job's Plea to God (10:1–22)

Once more Job turned to God directly in prayer, but his prayer is a lament and not praise. He asked for an explanation rather than for condemnation (10:2). In 10:3–7 Job questioned why God wanted to destroy that which he had created, unless God was like a man, bent on searching out Job's sins even though he knew Job was innocent. In 10:8–11 Job's description of his own creation by God is much like the description in Psalm 139:14–16.

Job's early life was marked by evidences of God's love and care (10:12), but now it seemed that all the while God was tricking or baiting him.

> Yet these [awful] things thou didst hide in my heart;
> I know that this was thy purpose.
>
> —10:13

Job believed that God's purpose all along was to make him suffer and to destroy him, that even during Job's happy days God had this end in mind. Here we see the depths to which Job's troubled mind had taken him. He believed that behind the smiling providence God hides a frowning face. He did not believe that "the best is yet to be—the last of life for which the first was made."

The subject of man's creation is introduced here for the

first time in the book of Job, although previously Eliphaz and Job had both discussed God's power over the sun, stars, and rain. There is much in Job about creation and nature. Creation and the natural world can tell us a great deal about God's eternal power and deity (Rom. 1:20), but God's love and grace can best be seen in his redemptive history. And Job knew little of God's redemptive acts in history.

In 10:16 Job accused God of hunting him like a lion and performing "wonders" (miracles) to make Job suffer so much. In 10:17 he said that God was always sending fresh supplies of troubles on him as a general sends fresh troops into the battle.

In 10:18 Job asked the question again: "Why was I born?" Then he repeated his wish that he had died at birth, "carried from the womb to the tomb!" (10:19). In 10:20–22 Job pleaded for God to let him alone so that he might have a little peace before he died and went to Sheol, which is a place "of gloom and deep darkness." Four different Hebrew words for darkness are used in this passage to describe Sheol.

Zophar—The Voice of Distilled Wisdom (11:1–20)

Rebukes Job for His Much Babbling (11:1–4)

One of the cruelest ways in which one man can attack another man is through ridicule—the refusal to recognize the sincerity and integrity of another. Job perhaps had been rash in some of his remarks, but he was serious. Now Zophar dismisses all of Job's questions and his claims of innocence as empty babblings and mockery.

Thinks Job Suffers Less Than He Deserves (11:5–6)

Job had complained that God would not speak to him (9:16). Now Zophar said that he wished God would speak to Job. If he did, Zophar was convinced that God would say that Job's punishment was less than he deserved.

Declares God's Wisdom and Man's Folly (11:7–12)

In 11:7–10, Zophar said that God's wisdom is unfathomable, therefore a man should not question God.

It is higher than heaven—what can you do?
  Deeper than Sheol—what can you know?
Its measure is longer than the earth,
  and broader than the sea.

—11:8–9

God knows man (11:11), but man is stupid or "hollow" and will get understanding "when a wild ass's colt is born a man" (11:12), which will never happen.

Calls for Job to Repent (11:13–20)

Zophar was convinced that Job had sinned. Therefore, almost flippantly, mechanically, and with no love or compassion he advised Job to repent (11:13–14). Then, Zophar believed, Job would automatically be restored. The darkness and gloom would vanish, and sunshine and security would be his (11:15–19). Then he fired one final warning at Job:

But the eyes of the wicked will fail;
all way of escape will be lost to them,
  and their hope is to breathe their last.

—11:20

Much of what Zophar said is true. God's nature and wisdom are unfathomable. Man can never know God fully. Paul said, "Now we see in a mirror dimly" (1 Cor. 13:12). Man is finite, and in spite of man's amazing discoveries and achievements in the last few years, he has only touched the hem of the garment of potential knowledge. Gheyselinck, in his book, *The Restless Earth,* said that if the whole history of the world from the Archaean Age until today were compressed into a film scheduled to run for twenty-four hours, "man would not appear until the last five seconds of the film!"[16] What can man know? God is great and wise. Man should repent. There are blessings for the righteous, and the wicked will not escape the judgment of God.

But Zophar made mistakes. He erred in not taking Job's questions seriously. Zophar should not have met Job's doubts with ridicule. Although Job's friend said that only God is wise, he seems to have considered himself an exception. Only he and God had the truth! Cromwell is reported to have said to Samuel Rutherford, whom he found very troublesome, "Have you ever considered the possibility that you might be mistaken?"

Zophar's attitude was wrong, and his solution was too simple. He felt that the only thing Job needed to do was to repent. And repentance *is* necessary for obedience to God. But Zophar failed to recognize that the physical, mental, and spiritual aspects of man's nature are bound up together, and a disorder in one area of one's life affects his total well-being. Have we advised people only to repent when we also should have told them to see a physician and/or a psychiatrist?

Job Speaks to Zophar, His Companions, and to God (12:1 to 14:22)

Job's Sarcastic Reply Concerning Man's Wisdom (12:1–12)

Zophar had reduced man's wisdom to nothing, but had acted as if he were all-wise. Job detected the implication that Zophar and his friends had a monopoly on wisdom and said:

> No doubt you are the people,
> and wisdom will die with you.
>
> —12:2

In 12:3 Job showed resentment of their arrogance and bigotry and said, "I am not inferior to you" (compare 13:2). Job's friends laughed at him and had contempt for him (12:4). Job said that it is easy for one who is at ease to have contempt for misfortune (12:5). The text of 12:6 is obscure, but it seems to refute what the friends had said about the wicked. Job asserted here that robbers have peace, and those who provoke God are secure. He was not aware of any provocation of God on his own part. He had provoked his friends but not God.

The expression, "who bring their god in their hand" (12:6) presents problems. The New English Bible omits it. Moffatt translates it, "who make a god of their own power." It is probably another example of Job's irony and means that if a man wants to command divine favor he must have a god he can control. In 12:7–12 Job said that wisdom like that displayed by his friends can be obtained by observing the animal and plant world or by listening to any old man.

Job's Ironical Description of God's Wisdom (12:13–25)

"Yes," Job said, "God is wise, but you never know what he is going to do!" God's power over men and nature is recognized, but Job said that it is not always a benevolent power. It seems that Job was deliberately emphasizing the negative aspects of God's power. When God tears down, none can rebuild; when he shuts a man in, none can open (12:14). If he withholds the waters, there is drought; if he sends out the waters there is a flood (12:15). He controls the strong and the wise; the deceived and the deceiver are both alike to him (12:16). For the Hebrew mind, God was behind all of the good and bad happenings in history (12:17–25).

Job believed in the sovereignty of God and the unfathomableness of divine wisdom, but he had problems reconciling his experiences and observations with his beliefs. In this, Job has his modern-day counterparts. We have difficulty seeing why divine wisdom allows some things. Perhaps we could learn from Oscar Wilde: "He was sure there was enough misery in one narrow London lane to disprove the notion that God is love. In later years when calamity after its kind overtook him, he seemed equally sure that love of some sort is the only possible explanation of the extraordinary amount of suffering in the world. The story of human existence can be read both ways." [17]

Job Argues with God (13:1–19)

Job had some harsh words for his friends in 13:1–12. He had first addressed his questions to them, thinking that they might be able to help him, but they only offered him worn-out clichés and useless half-truths.

> Your maxims are proverbs of ashes,
> your defenses are defenses of clay.
>
> —13:12

Job accused his friends of whitewashing or smearing over the truth of being worthless physicians (13:4). He said they would be wise if they kept their mouths shut, but instead of keeping silent they felt called to defend God. In reality, they were defending their own theology, not God. Job accused his friends of lying for God!

> Will you speak falsely for God,
> and speak deceitfully for him?
>
> —13:7

Job warned his comforters to beware of the justice of God. A lie in defense of God is no less a lie. God will rebuke those who speak deceitfully for him (13:7–11). God can take care of himself; and when we try to defend him, we run the risk of re-creating him in our image.

Job had argued with his friends; he was now ready to argue with God. The unsatisfactory results of his discussion with his friends caused Job to "take his flesh in his teeth" and "his life in his hand." He would go boldly into the presence of God and have it out with him (13:13–14). To barge unbidden into the presence of an Oriental king often meant death. Job knew that death might be the result of his proposed course of action. His attitude was much like that of the four lepers at the gate of Samaria who, as they decided to go into the Syrian camp, said, "If they kill us we shall but die" (2 Kings 7:4). Job was determined to pursue his quest. He said:

> Behold, he will slay me; I have no hope;
> yet I will defend my ways to his face.
>
> —13:15

Many readers will remember that the first part of this verse in the King James Version is translated, "Though he slay me, yet will I trust in him." That is a noble thought and one that fits Job's experience much of the time. But that is not precisely what Job said at this point. The context presents Job as getting ready to go into the presence of God. He has little hope that he will come out alive. But defending his integrity before God seemed a better way to die than by cursing God and dying, as his wife had suggested.

The King James Version used a marginal Hebrew reading;

the Revised Standard Version uses the regular Hebrew text. (Compare New English Bible.) For a moment Job evidenced a glimmer of hope when he said, "This shall be my salvation, that a godless man [not a hypocrite] shall not come before him" (13:16) and, "I know that I shall be vindicated" (13:18).

Job's Two Requests of God (13:20–27)

Job actually had not encountered God at this point in his experience. He was just practicing what he would say to God if he had the opportunity. He made two requests of God. He asked, "withdraw thy hand far from me" (compare 9:34; 33:7); and he invited God to enter into dialogue with him (13:22).

Then Job had a long list of questions he would ask God: How many sins had Job committed? What were they? Why did God hide his face? Why did God count Job as his enemy? Why did God, who has unlimited power, overwhelm Job as a driven leaf or a bit of dry chaff? Why did he write bitter things against Job and make him inherit the sins of his youth? Why did God keep Job in chains and spy on him all of the time? Why did God put an identifying mark on the soles of Job's feet?

Man's Mortality (13:28 to 14:12)

Death occupies a large place in the book of Job. We do not know the nature of Job's illness, but no doubt it was serious enough to cause him to reflect upon death many times. In chapter 3 Job prayed to die, not because of the attractiveness of his view of life after death, but because it promised him release from his present suffering. Death is presented as a normal occurrence for an old man in 5:26, but it is never presented as something to be desired ahead of time.

In 13:28 to 14:12 Job reflected on man's mortality. Man is compared to a rotten thing, a moth-eaten garment, a withering flower, and a fleeing shadow. The expression "born of woman" marks the common lot of man as one of frailty, sorrow, and possibly as a participant in the common sinfulness of man. The sinfulness of the race seems to be acknowledged by Job in 14:4 as it was expounded by Eliphaz in 4:17–18, and (later) 15:14–15, and in Psalm 51:5.

Job 14:4 has been considered by some a marginal gloss that has crept into the text by mistake. It is not in one Hebrew manuscript and the New English Bible omits it from the text and puts it in a footnote. But there is no real reason for considering this verse as spurious. Perhaps it should be read as the expression of a deep desire: "O that a clean thing could come out of an unclean one. None can" (14:4). Job nowhere claimed to be sinless. He did argue that the enormity of his suffering was not justified on the basis of the enormity of his sin. In fact, in this passage Job seems to have been pleading for God's mercy on the basis of his share in the sinfulness of the race.

In 14:7–12 Job contrasted the fate of a man with that of a tree. He said that there is more hope for a tree to live again than there is for a man. When a tree is cut down new growth usually sprouts from the stump. But man dies and vanishes completely like water that has evaporated in a dry lake or empty river bed. There is no loss more final or less recoverable than water that has soaked into the dry earth. Job's picture of death is one of its impressive finality. Zophar had used the figure of the vanishing water to describe the fleeting nature of misery (11:16); here Job used it to refer to the finality of death.

Perhaps it was this understanding of the finality of death that made the people of Israel prefer life here and now in any form to whatever may be on the other side of death. Job said to God:

> Look away from him, and desist,
> that he may enjoy, like a hireling, his day.
> —14:6

Dostoevsky makes Raskolnikov say in *Crime and Punishment:*

> Life is only given to me and I shall never have it again; I don't want to wait for "the happiness of all." I want to live myself, or else better not to live at all. . . . Where is it I've read that someone condemned to death says or

thinks, an hour before his death, that if he had to live on some high rock, or such a narrow ledge, that he'd only have room to stand, and the ocean, everlasting darkness, everlasting solitude, everlasting tempest around him, if he had to remain standing on a square yard of space all his life, a thousand years, eternity, it were better to live so than to die at once! Only to live, to live and live! Life, whatever it may be! . . . How true it is! Good God how true! [18]

A Glimmer of Hope (14:13–15)

The first flash of light broke through Job's darkness when he expressed the impossible wish that God would hide him (Job) in Sheol until God's wrath is passed, then recall him to life and fellowship again (14:13). In 14:14 Job asked, "If a man die, shall he live again?" He said that if that were possible he would gladly endure all of the suffering and shame that was his lot in anticipation that some day God would remember "the work of his hands," and call for Job and Job would answer, "Here am I, Lord" (14:15).

Job's Present and Future Still Dark (14:16–22)

Verses 16 and 17 are probably expressions of despair rather than hope. The Revised Standard Version and Moffatt take them as a continuation of Job's hope. But the King James Version, the American Standard Version, Smith-Goodspeed, and the New English Bible take them as a return to the thought that God is spying on Job. God has sealed up Job's sins to use against him. God determines all of Job's steps (14:16–17; compare 14:5).

Some of the most pessimistic words in the book are found in 14:18–22. Job had rejected the idea that there might be a meaningful life after death, and in beautiful but sad language described the fate of one for whom there is no hope of resurrection:

> But the mountain falls and crumbles away,
>   and the rock is removed from its place;
> the waters wear away the stones;
>   the torrents wash away the soil of the earth;
>   so thou destroyest the hope of man.

Thou prevailest for ever against him, and he passes;
 thou changest his countenance, and sendest him away.
 —14:18–20

Often in the ancient world men found consolation concerning the future in the belief that men live on in their children. This doctrine held that if man cannot live forever, perhaps he can continue to live through his son or sons. Job considered that possibility and found it unsatisfactory also, not because Job's sons were dead but because when a man dies he has no more consciousness of what goes on on earth (14:21–22). An opposite view of this pessimistic idea is stated in Hebrews 12:1.

So ends the first argument. Viewpoints have been stated. Tempers have flared. Polarity has developed between Job and his friends, but Job's chief concern still was the hiddenness of God. It is fortunate for us that the biblical writer did not stop at this point in the book.

---

1. H. L. Ellison, *From Tragedy to Triumph*, p. 36.
2. T. H. Robinson, *Job and His Friends* (London: SCM Press, Ltd, 1954), p. 62. Used by permission.
3. H. L. Ellison, *op. cit.*, p. 42.
4. James Moffatt, *The Bible* (New York: Harper and Brothers, 1935). Used by permission.
5. Franz Delitzsch, *The Book of Job* (Edinburgh: T. and T. Clark, 1866), p. 114.
6. J. M. P. Smith and Edgar J. Goodspeed, *An American Translation of the Bible* (Chicago: The University of Chicago Press, 1949). Used by permission.
7. *The New English Bible* © The Delegates of the Oxford University Press and the Syndics of the Cambridge University Press, 1961, 1970. This and all other quotations marked NEB are used by permission.
8. Marvin Pope, *Job* "The Anchor Bible" (Garden City, New York: Doubleday and Company, 1965), p. 19.
9. H. L. Ellison, *op. cit.*, p. 38.
10. Pope, *op. cit.*, p. 61.
11. James Wood, *Job and the Human Situation* (London: Geoffrey Bles, 1966), p. 54. Used by permission.
12. James A. Froude, *The Voice Out of the Whirlwind: The Book of Job*. Edited by Ralph E. Hone (San Francisco: Chandler Publishing Co., 1960), p. 205.
13. H. L. Ellison, *op. cit.*, p. 42.

14. See James D. Bryden, *God and Human Suffering* (Nashville: Broadman Press, 1965), p. 57.

15. See Leslie D. Weatherhead, *Salute to a Sufferer* (New York: Abingdon Press, 1962), p. 46. Used by permission.

16. Weatherhead, *op. cit.*, p. 57.

17. Interpreter's Bible, *op. cit.*, p. 1000.

18. See Samuel Terrien, *Job: Poet of Existence* (Indianapolis: The Bobbs-Merrill Co., 1957), p. 60. Reprinted by permission of the publisher.

5

The Second Argument:
The Fate of the Wicked

(15:1 to 21:34)

THE MAJOR THEME of the second argument between Job and his friends is the fate of the wicked. At least this is the theme of the three friends. They pursue the subject with considerable zeal. (See 15:17–35; 18:1–21; 20:1–29.) It does not appear at first that Job was very interested in the wicked man's fate. In his first and second speeches of this cycle, Job continued to bemoan his plight and to consider God his enemy (16:6 to 17:16; 19:1–29). However, a high point of faith and commitment was reached near the end of his second speech when he said, "I know that my Redeemer lives." In that moment, Job was released, at least temporarily, from his personal problems to discuss the fate of the wicked in his third speech (21:1–34).

Eliphaz' Second Speech: Job Is Undermining Religion (15:1–35)

Job Is No Wise Man (15:1–16)

Job had claimed to be as wise as his comforters (12:3; 13:2). Eliphaz set out to refute that claim. In verses 2 and 3 he said that if Job were wise he would not be so windy or wordy (compare 8:2; 11:2). Then Eliphaz accused Job of irreverence and heresy:

> But you are doing away with the fear of God,
> and hindering meditation before God.
>
> —15:4

Eliphaz felt that Job was a threat to traditional religion. He thought Job's charges against God would be a stumbling block for many people. Job was rocking the theological boat. Therefore, Eliphaz appointed himself guardian of the people less wise than himself, to protect them from Job's blasphemy and heresy. The root of Job's trouble, according to Eliphaz, was a wicked heart, "Your iniquity teaches your mouth." According to Eliphaz, Job was not wise, but crafty (15:5). Job was turning the spotlight away from himself by accusing God and his friends of wrong. Eliphaz condemned Job on the basis of Job's own testimony. He hurled this piercing pronouncement at Job:

> Your own mouth condemns you, and not I;
> Your own lips testify against you.
>
> —15:6

Job had no opportunity to refuse to testify further. Eliphaz had heard all he needed to hear. He saw no need for further investigation. No other witnesses needed to be called. Job was guilty. His own mouth condemned him. Such a conclusion reminds us of the words of high priest, "Why do we still need witnesses?" (Mark 14:63).

So far as Eliphaz was concerned, Job was not a wise man, because he was not old enough, and because he had not stood in the council of God (15:7–8). According to Eliphaz, wisdom only comes with age (note 12:12; 32:7–9). We do not know the ages of Eliphaz and Job. Job was probably an adult in early maturity, since he refers to himself fourteen times as a *gebher* "strong man." Even though he had ten children, none of them seems to have been married at the time of their death. Eliphaz was probably quite a bit older than Job. Of course, Eliphaz had even older associates.

> Both the grayhaired and the aged are among us,
> older than your father. —15:10

With exaggerated sarcasm, Eliphaz asked Job if he were the first man to be born. Did Job have exclusive access to the secret council of God?

Again Eliphaz asserted Job was not wise because he considered "the consolations of God" too small and rejected the word that dealt gently with him (15:11). What Eliphaz called the "consolations of God" probably were the words of Eliphaz' dream in 4:17–21. He considered his words the words of God. And "the word that dealt gently with Job" (15:11) probably refers to Eliphaz' first speech, which was delivered in a rather gentle fashion.

Finally, Job was not wise because according to his accuser, he had turned against God; and, if God puts no trust in his angels, how much less will he trust "one who is abominable, and corrupt, a man who drinks iniquity like water" (15:12–16). As Eliphaz saw it, Job was exceedingly guilty and unwise.

The Fate of the Wicked (15:17–35)

Eliphaz based his view of the fate of the wicked on what he had seen (15:17) and on the unadulterated traditions of the fathers (15:18–19). Job had perhaps unconsciously challenged the theology of his friends by saying that the wicked often prosper and do not suffer (9:24; 10:3; 12:6).

> The earth is given into the hand of the wicked;
> he covers the faces of its judges—
> if it is not he, who then is it?
> —9:24

> Does it seem good to thee to oppress,
> to despise the work of thy hands
> and favor the designs of the wicked?
> —10:3

> The tents of robbers are at peace,
> and those who provoke God are secure,
> who bring their god in their hand.
> —12:6

Eliphaz replied that Job's claim only seems to be true at times. In reality, asserted Eliphaz, the wicked suffer all of the time. If they do not suffer outwardly, they suffer pains of conscience. The wicked always hear terrifying sounds and live in constant fear (15:20–23). The wicked man's fear is due to his defiance of the Almighty, "running stubbornly against him with a thick-bossed shield" (15:25–26). Job reversed this image in his next speech and made God run against him (16:14).

Eliphaz pictured the wicked man as covering his face with his fat. Fatness in the Old Testament is often a picture of dulness, gross insensitivity, and even rebellion, which prosperity often brings (see Deut. 32:15; Isa. 6:10; Jer. 5:27–28; Ps. 73:7). It is not quite clear (15:28) why the wicked man lived in desolate cities. This is probably a reference to those who defied God in rebuilding cities, such as Jericho or Babylon, which had been put under the ban (Josh. 6:26; I Kings 16:34; Deut. 13:16; Isa. 13:19–20; 34:10).

Job 15:29–35 is a graphic picture of the fate of a wicked man. He will not be rich or stable (15:29). Nothing but darkness, barrenness, emptiness, and premature death await him (15:30–34). The wicked conceive mischief and bring forth deceit (15:35; Ps. 7:14; Isa. 33:11; 59:4). In this speech, Eliphaz made no attempt to comfort Job. Instead his object seems to have been to warn and to frighten him.

Job's Second Reply to Eliphaz and a Brief prayer (16:1 to 17:16)

His Friends Are Miserable Comforters (16:1–5)

Job was getting used to his friends by this time. After Eliphaz' second speech, Job asserted that he found nothing new in it, "I have heard many such things [before]" (16:2). Then he reminded them that they had come originally to comfort him (16:2; 2:11). Having failed in that noble purpose, their windy words should have an end (16:3). Job said that it does not take a wise man to do what the friends were doing: "join words together" and shake their heads at Job (16:4). But, said he, if their roles were reversed—if they were on the ash heap and he in good health—he would strengthen them and assuage their pain with his words (16:4–5). But it was not his friends that most concerned Job at this point. It was God. Job still thought God was his enemy.

Is God Still His Enemy (16:6–14)?

Job was in a bitter mood. He believed that it made no difference whether he spoke or did not speak. On a number of occasions Job reminds us of Henley's "Invictus":

> Out of the night that covers me,
> Black as the Pit from pole to pole,
> I thank whatever gods may be
> For my unconquerable soul.

Job was aware of the truth that God is and that he is one, but the tormented man's night was still black and his soul unconquerable. It seemed to Job that God had exhausted his strength and patience, and deprived him of his family and friends (16:7). God had shriveled him up (a reference to his disease). His condition testified to the world that he was a sinner (16:8). Job said that like a wild beast God "has torn me in his wrath, . . . gnashed his teeth at me," and "sharpened his eye against me" (16:9).

Job seems to have been calling God his adversary in 16:9. However, he may have been referring to men, whom he described in 16:10 as gaping at him with their mouths, striking him on the cheek and massing themselves together against him (Ps. 22:12–13; Isa. 57:4). Job felt that God had given him over to the hands of the ungodly (16:11). In 16:12 Job again took up his theme that God was his enemy. Perhaps referring to his former days Job said:

> I was at ease, and he broke me asunder;
> he seized me by the neck and dashed me to pieces;
> he set me up as his target,
> his archers surround me.
> He slashed open my kidneys, and does not spare;
> he pours out my gall on the ground.
> He breaks me with breach upon breach;
> he runs upon me like a warrior.
>
> —16:12–14

Job Humbled but Not Cast Down (16:15–17)

This may be the turning point in Job's experience. He said that he had put sackcloth on his skin and laid his strength in the dust. Pride had been a part of Job's problem. Now he was beginning the journey of the surrender of self. He did not give up his claim to integrity (16:17), but he was beginning to lay aside his reliance upon himself. He reminds us of the apostle Paul who later said: "We are afflicted in every way, but not crushed; perplexed, but not driven to despair; persecuted, but not forsaken; struck down, but not destroyed" (2 Cor. 4:8–9).

Job's Witness Is in Heaven (16:18 to 17:2)

Job felt that he was about to meet an unjust fate. He was going to be murdered. He expressed this thought in the words, "O earth, cover not my blood, and let my cry find no resting place" (16:18). Only the shed blood of a murder victim had to be avenged. If a person died justly or naturally his blood needed no avenging. According to the belief of the ancients, innocent blood cried out from the ground until it was covered (Gen. 4:10; Ezek. 24:7). Job envisioned his innocent blood spilled, with no human avenger and with no earthly witness for him. Then in a leap of faith and in a moment of inspiration Job claims:

> Even now, behold my witness is in heaven,
> and he that vouches for me is on high.
>
> —16:19

Job had given up on his "friends" on earth. There was no other place to turn except heaven. He did not identify his "witness." Many people have assumed that Job was speaking of God as his witness, but that is by no means a certainty. Job may have been taking up Eliphaz' question in 5:1, "To which one of the holy ones will you turn?" Job may have thought that since angels are higher than man they should be able to see right and wrong more clearly than man. If no man recognized Job's integrity and was willing to be a witness for him, surely there was one in heaven who would be a witness for him. Perhaps Job was building on his own suggestion in 9:33 that there should be an umpire between man and God. Now Job believed that there could be such an umpire in heaven. This umpire would be a witness for him and would maintain his right before God.

Terrien wrote of this "witness": Job is "beginning to lift the veil from the mystery of the Godhead. He does not indicate whether the **witness** is a divine being, 'a son of Elohim' (cf. 1:6), a 'servant' or 'messenger' (cf. 4:18), or again a 'holy one' (cf. 15:15). By presenting the figure of the witness and by respecting the anonymity of that figure, he [Job] reopens the theme of the mediator (9:33), prepares the motif of the redeemer (19:25), and thus lays the basis of Christian mediation [sic]." [1] Scherer, in the same volume, wrote that of Job's statement in verse 19: "The phoenix of a new faith is rising out of the ashes." [2]

In this passage, the Christian can see clearly the picture of a man who cries out for that intercession which even now our Lord provides for the redeemed. In Job's day and in ours, the heart of man seeks someone who will "maintain his right, who will speak up for him in his hour of need."

The Hebrew word translated "maintain his right" (16:21) comes from the same root as the word translated "umpire" in 9:33. The heavenly umpire had now become a "maintainer" of Job's rights. Job's friends scorned him for entertaining such an idea (16:20). His eyes continued to pour out tears to God, for in a "few years" (a short time) Job was going the way of no return (16:22). His spirit was broken, and the grave was ready for him. Mockers were all about him (17:1–2).

A Brief Prayer (17:3–5)

In every speech in the first cycle Job turned from his friends to God. This is not true in the last two cycles. This passage is a brief prayer, but even it is a kind of a challenge to God. Job asked God to go on his bond or to put up bail for him because there was no one else willing to do it. God had closed Job's friends' minds against him. Surely God would not allow them to triumph (17:3–5).

Job: a Righteous Byword, a Kinsman to Worms (17:6–16)

Again Job bemoaned his situation. He had become a byword, and many people spat at him. He had almost cried his eyes out, and his body was like a skeleton (17:6–7). Some few upright men were appalled at his plight, but he himself grew stronger and stronger in his conviction that he was righteous.

> My eye has grown dim from grief,
> and all my members are like a shadow.
> Upright men are appalled at this,
> and the innocent stirs himself up against the godless.
> Yet the righteous holds to his way,
> and he that has clean hands grows stronger and stronger.
> —17:7–9

A. B. Davidson called 17:9 "perhaps the most surprising and lofty passage in the book." Franz Delitzsch compared it to "a rocket which shoots above the tragic darkness of the book." Other interpreters have argued that the verse is out of place here because the next few verses present a dark, hopeless picture. Perhaps Job was asserting his righteousness in spite of the fact that he did not share the hope, held out by his friends, of a speedy recovery for the righteous. Job felt that his death could not be far away. Ironically, he referred to the pit and the worm in endearing terms:

> If I say to the pit, "You are my father,"
> and to the worm, "My mother," or "My sister,"
> where then is my hope?
> Who will see my hope?
> —17:14–15

Bildad's Second Speech (18:1–21)

Personal Remarks to Job (and Friends) (18:1–4)

It is not clear whether Bildad was addressing Job individually or whether he was including others (perhaps Eliphaz and Zophar) in his opening remarks. The Septuagint uses singular pronouns in verses 2 and 4. Bildad accused Job (and his friends) of looking for new forms of rhetoric without really considering the issues or debating them (18:2). In 12:7 Job had said to his friends that the beasts could teach them wisdom. So in 18:3 Bildad asked Job why he counted his friends beasts and stupid ("vile," KJV). Bildad informed Job that his friends were not beasts, but that Job was tearing himself in his anger like a beast (18:4). (In 16:9, Job had accused God of tearing him apart like a beast.)

The real question Bildad had to ask Job is in 18:4:

> Shall the earth be forsaken for you
> or the rock be removed out of its place?

This question is subject to various interpretations, but it probably refers to a complete reversal of the created order. The friends considered the operation of moral law inherent in the universe to be irrevocable. According to the theology of Job's friends, to admit that suffering such as Job's could come upon the righteous would be tantamount to turning creation upside down. Did Job think he was so important that the laws of God would be miraculously reversed on his account?

The Light of the Wicked Will Be Put Out (18:5–21)

Bildad graphically portrayed the tragic fate that awaits the wicked. The light within him is put out. All joy and meaning are removed from existence for the wicked (18:5). Then the light of his tent and his surroundings becomes dark (18:6). His confident, strong strides become short, cautious steps, and his own schemes make him fall (18:7). He is ensnared by the traps of evil he has set for himself. Terrors surround him and dog his steps (18:11). Calamity and disease tear him away from his tent and march him to the king of terrors (death). His tent is taken over by another who is none of his; brimstone is scattered upon his habitation (18:15).

Job 18:15 is very difficult. The Anchor Bible reconstructs it on the basis of modern Ugaritic * discoveries:

---

* This refers to clay tablets discovered in 1929 in the Northern Syrian coasts. These seem to date back to the fourteenth century B.C. These tablets shed light on Old Testament phrases and hitherto obscure words. The discoveries help to clarify our knowledge of the world in which Israel developed.

> Fire is set in his tent,
> on his abode is scattered brimstone.[8]

The New English Bible has this:

> Magic herbs lie strewn about his tent
> and his home is sprinkled with sulphur to protect it.

In 18:16 the figure of the total destruction of a tree—roots and branches—is used to describe the total destruction of the wicked. Bildad was probably thinking of Job's reference to the hope that a tree, when it is cut down, will sprout again (14:7). Bildad declared that such is not true in the case of the wicked. Memory of him will perish from the earth (18:17). He will be driven from the light into darkness (18:18). Bildad again referred to the absence of children and survivors of the wicked (18:19).

The last two verses of chapter 18 are also difficult. Bildad had just said the wicked will not be remembered (18:17). Now he seems to say that the fate of the wicked will be known universally (from East to West) or eternally ("they that come after and they who went before," KJV). Perhaps what Bildad was saying is that nothing good will be remembered about the wicked. He will have no mourners or survivors; only the memory of his tragic end will continue.

Job's Second Reply to Bildad: "I Know My Redeemer Lives" (19:1–29)

This is one of the great chapters of the Bible because in it Job expresses his certainty that eventually he will be vindicated, even if it must be after he dies. Men will know that he is "perfect" [blameless] as God said he was (1:8), and he will see God for himself.

There are two main difficulties in interpreting this chapter: The Hebrew text of the chapter is uncertain in many places—this is true most of all in verse 25–27, the very place where Job's great confession of faith is found. The uncertainty in the Hebrew manuscripts and ancient versions is probably due to the fact that these verses were the battleground for or against the doctrine of the resurrection between factions of later Judaism and between Judaism and

Christianity. A second reason why this passage is difficult to interpret is because it is virtually impossible for the Christian to keep from reading into it his own concepts of redemption and resurrection. But we do not have to deny its ultimate meaning for us in order to approach first the passage from Job's vantage point. (More on v. 25 follows.)

Job's Retort to His Friends (19:1–5)

Job asked his friends how long they would torment him and crush him with their words (19:1). He tried to shame them, and then he accused them of casting a reproach on him ten times (a round number for "often"). They had accused Job of error. He said that if their accusation were true (which it was not) his sin should not concern them (19:4). It is not clear whether Job was saying that his sin would be none of his friends' business or saying that he should be conscious of any sins he had committed, and he was unaware of any.

Job accused his friends of having an ulterior motive in bringing charges against him. He charged that they were accusing him of sin in order to magnify themselves (19:5).

God Had Imprisoned Him, and Taken Away His Justice and Honor (19:6–12)

In words similar to those in chapters 9, 13, and 17, Job blamed God for his plight. He cried, "Murder!" but no one came to his rescue (19:7). God had closed a net about him (19:6). God had walled up Job's way, set darkness on his path, stripped away his glory and crown, pulled up his hope like a tree, and sent troops to besiege his tent (19:8–12).

Job Has No Human Vindicator (19:13–22)

Here is one of the most poignant pictures of human loneliness and ostracism to be found in all of literature. Job was probably forced to move out of the city to the ash heap when he contracted his disease. At first some of his friends kept coming to see him, but finally he became totally estranged from society. Terrien says of verses 13–19, "The phrases unroll without pause, and the emotion wells up as an orchestral crescendo upon a monotone (13–19)." [4]

Notice the various groups that Job listed who might have

been his vindicators or at least his friends but had all with one accord abandoned him: brethren, acquaintances, kinsfolk, close friends, guests in his house, his servant, his wife, the sons of his mother, little children, and even intimate friends whom he loved. The last word is the saddest of all. Job spoke of loving some of his friends (perhaps Eliphaz, Bildad, and Zophar), and he probably thought they loved him. But instead of responding in love to him in his suffering, they chided and condemned.

Job described his feeling of isolation in the graphic expression, "I have escaped by the skin of my teeth" (19:20). In words which remind us of Psalm 51:1, Job called for his friends to have mercy or pity upon him, for the hand of God had touched him.

Job's Appeal to the Future (19:23–29)

Out of the depths of great sorrow and loneliness, Job began to rise to his greatest heights of belief and anticipation. He began by expressing the wish that his words might be written down in a book; perhaps inscribed on a copper scroll. There is some question about verse 23. What "words" did Job want inscribed in a book or on a rock? Was it his confession in verse 25, "I know that my Redeemer lives"? Or, was it his words about his innocence? It was probably the latter. Job wanted his name cleared and his honor vindicated. He had given up hope of such being done during his lifetime. Therefore, he thought of some way of preserving his case to be decided by posterity. He wanted some permanent record to be made of it either on metal scroll or on a rock. He did not want his case to be buried in a book or hidden in some obscure inscription. He wanted a personal advocate—someone who would go to bat for him, clear his name, and reconcile him and God.

Then in a flash of light as brilliant as the noonday sun, Job exclaimed, "for [but] I know that my Redeemer lives!" Every word in that sentence is emphatic. The "but" is more than a conjunctive. It introduces verse 25 as something different from what has gone before. In effect, Job said, "I could wish for my case to be written in a book or on a rock, *but* there is something better than that; namely, a living Redeemer." The pronoun "I" is emphatic here in Hebrew. The word "know" is a regular word which means "to know by experience."

The word "redeemer" in verse 25 is the Hebrew word, *go'el.* It is used of a man, the next of kin, who acts as the avenger of blood in the case of a murder. It is used for the redeemer of a kinsman who has been sold into slavery. In some cases the *go'el* redeemed the property of his kinsman and married his widow to raise up children to bear his name. (Compare Ruth 2:20; 3:9; 4:4.) Sometimes God is called Israel's *Go'el* (Ex. 6:6; 15:13; Ps. 74:2; Isa. 41:14; 43:1).

Was Job here speaking of a human *go'el* or of a divine *Go'el?* It seems that he had given up all hope in man's ability and willingness to justify him. He turned toward heaven, but God was his enemy (he thought). He believed that God was responsible for all of his trouble (which is true in a sense). Therefore, Job returned to his earlier thoughts of an umpire (9:33) and a heavenly witness (16:19). He advanced to the concept of a living Redeemer (19:25), a "vindicator." The kind of redeemer Job envisioned would have to be one who would not die, as he was about to do, but who would at last "stand upon the earth (dust)." Even after Job died such a Redeemer would usher him into the presence of God, where from his flesh he would see God (19:26).

Who was this Redeemer of Job's? What kind of redemption was Job speaking of? How would this redemption be accomplished? These questions have been answered in a myriad of ways. Some say that Job was thinking of God as his Redeemer (see Balmer Kelly, Peake's Commentary, A. B. Davidson, H. L. Ellison). Others say that Job was still looking for a human redeemer. Through many centuries there have been commentators who saw here a full-blown reference to the Messiah. These men argued that Job saw Jesus' day and was glad. But that view does not seem to fit all of the facts in Job's case. Such a view would seem to be inconsistent with his expressions of pessimism in the later chapters. If Job had really foreseen what God would do in Christ, could he have been anything but joyfully optimistic?

Perhaps the best interpretation is to see in the references

to the umpire, heavenly witness, and living Redeemer, an almost unconscious outreach of Job's mind and heart to the reality of a mediator between God and man. The need was there. God is God and man is man. They exist on different planes. Job's experience of suffering, combined with his own sense of blamelessness and his friends' charges that he had sinned grievously, caused him to turn to God. But Job thought God was his enemy. Therefore, he saw only one other alternative, a God-man—who later fully revealed himself in the person of Jesus Christ.

What kind of Redeemer was Job expecting? At this point he was not expecting one who would redeem him from sin, for he was still asserting his innocence. He was expecting a kinsman redeemer who would clear his good name before God so that he might see God and be reconciled to him.

How did Job expect the redeemer to accomplish his redemption? Again we need a reminder that the text is very problematical, and we cannot operate in this area with absolute certainly. But it seems that Job expected to die soon. He felt that after death, his redeemer would stand (or appear) over the dust of his grave (19:25), and would call God and Job together. Job would see God for himself on his side. It would be no secondhand report (compare 42:5). Such a thought was almost too much for Job, "My heart faints within me!" (19:27).

Was Job setting out a doctrine of the resurrection? Handel in his famous oratorio, *Messiah*, began his third section, which deals with the resurrection, with this passage from Job. But at this point, we cannot say that Job was asserting that there would be a general resurrection. He did not make a clear claim that he would live forever. He asserted his belief that if he died before his problem was solved, death would be no final barrier. He felt that eventually his case would be righted and he himself would see God.

Job had made two tremendous discoveries. Or, to put it another way, God had revealed two tremendous concepts to Job: Death does not have to be a barrier to faith or fellowship with God; man may have to wait until after he dies for explanations for some things. Also, Job could not vindicate himself;

he needed a living redeemer, and he had one in heaven.

What difference did this experience have in Job's life? Did he stay on the mountaintop, or did he fall back into the valley below? Some seem to think that this great confession of faith had little or no effect on the later speeches of Job.

James Wood said: "He must journey on without the light from heaven. For him, the human situation is dark with the shadows of doubt and despair." [5]

Balmer Kelly wrote, "This height is not maintained hereafter in unwavering and continuous faith." [6]

But T. H. Robinson said: "From this point onwards there is a remarkable change in the tone of Job's speeches. The emotional tension slackens, and even the bitterness of the friends makes comparatively little impression on Job. Of course Job does not wholly ignore them, still less can he escape questions raised by his sufferings and the problem of meeting God. But in ch. 21 he is able, for the first time, to take a fairly calm and dispassionate view of the general problem." [7]

Job's confidence in a vindicator made him bold so that he carried the war into the enemies' camp. His friends probably could hardly believe their ears when Job said:

> If you say, "How we will pursue him!"
>   and, "The root of the matter is found in him";
> be afraid of the sword,
>   for wrath brings the punishment of the sword,
>   that you may know there is a judgment.
>
> 19:28–29

Zophar's Second Speech (21:1–29)

Insulted Zophar Makes Rapid Reply (20:1–3)

Again Zophar reminds us of Elihu (32:19–20). He was bursting to speak before Job finished his last discourse. Job accused his friends of tormenting him and breaking him in pieces with words (19:2). He said that they had reproached him so many times they should be ashamed of themselves (19:3). Job asked why they kept on pursuing him (19:22), and he threatened them with the sword of judgment (19:

28–29). Job's claim of a living redeemer had unsettled Zophar's thoughts a little, but he quickly recovered his orthodox balance. He found a ready traditional answer, so that he would not have to deal with a new theological thought.

Paul Scherer says of Zophar's speech:

> Zophar has been unable to make heads or tails out of Job's reply to Bildad. . . . He cannot fit into his ready-made scheme of things such undisciplined imaginings, or what would come of them if they were true. So he puts together his jig-saw puzzle with the pieces that make sense to him—the kind of sense he can belabor with all his might—and pays no attention to the others, simply lays them over to one side. The trouble is that the other pieces are the key pieces: his bewildered friend's innocence, the obvious inequities of human existence, and the incredible madness toward which the tortured soul of Job is being driven.
>
> . . . .
>
> Manifestly, the technique is ready at hand for all comparable situations. Dismiss what you cannot manage, turn a deaf ear to the very heart of the matter if you cannot still its beating. Then fight back with all the vehemence you can muster.[8]

Zophar Claims the Prosperity of the Wicked Is Brief (20:4–11)

Zophar admitted that a wicked man may prosper briefly but he also perishes quickly and completely. In 20:4–5 he appealed to the past to prove that the exulting of the wicked is short and the joy of the godless but for a moment. Contrast this view of the brevity of the joy of the godless with the brevity of weeping in Psalm 30:5:

> For his anger is but for a moment,
> and his favor is for a lifetime.
> Weeping may tarry for the night,
> but joy comes with the morning.

Zophar continued to paint a dark picture of the wicked man's fate. Perhaps he was in part refuting Job's claim of a heavenly redeemer when he said of the wicked man:

Though his height mount up to the heavens,
  and his head reach to the clouds,
he will perish for ever like his own dung;
  those who have seen him will say,
    "Where is he?"
He will fly away like a dream, and not be found;
  he will be chased away like a vision of the night.
—20:6–8

Zophar claimed that the prosperity of the wicked does not endure. The children of the wicked become paupers, and he is cut off in the prime of life (20:10–11).

Sweetness Soon Becomes Bitterness (20:12–18)

Zophar compared wickedness to a tasty morsel which a man rolls around with his tongue, holding it in his mouth as long as possible in order to extract the last bit of sweetness out of it before swallowing it (20:12–13). When he swallows, the wickedness becomes poison, and he vomits all the riches he has swallowed. He will no more look upon rivers of milk and honey. "He will give back the fruit of his toil" (20:17–18).

The Insatiable Greed of the Wicked (20:19–29)

Perhaps with one eye on Job, Zophar accused the wicked man of crushing the poor and seizing houses he did not build, "because his greed knew no rest." (Compare Amos 2:7; 5:11; 8:4.)

Zophar (20:23) asserted that God repays the wicked for all his sins—good measure, pressed down, running over. God will fill the wicked man's belly full of his fierce anger. The wicked will flee from a spear or sword only to have his body pierced with an arrow (20:24–25). He will be hounded by terrors. "Utter darkness is laid up for his treasures" (20:26). "A fire not blown" [possibly God's fire] will devour him" (see 1:16). Instead of heaven revealing Job's innocence as he asserted in 19:25, it would reveal his iniquity, and men would rise up against him (20:27). In Zophar's view, all of this would be according to the decree of God. Zophar ended his speech with a word of warning as Job had done (19:28–29).

Job's Rebuttal: The Wicked Prosper (21:1–34)

In no other part of the dialogue do we find such an attempt to refute specific arguments of the previous speaker as we do in this chapter. Job's previous confession that he was certain that his living redeemer would vindicate him seems to have freed him from despair, for the moment at least. Now he could give his attention to his friend's argument that sinners always suffer grief and loss.

Attention Please! (21:1–6)

Job called for the undivided attention of his friends and said that in that way they could become true comforters indeed! Job felt he had a right to ask for silence because actually his friends should lay their hands upon their mouths and be appalled at him as they saw his suffering (21:3–5). Every time he allowed himself to reflect on his situation his flesh shuddered (21:6).

The Wicked's Fortune (21:7–13)

Job's statements here are a contradiction of everything Zophar had said about the fate of the wicked. "Just look," Job said in effect. The wicked do not die in the prime of life (20:11) but grow old and mighty in power (21:7). Their children do not become paupers (20:10) but are well established (21:8). Their houses or tents are not consumed (20:26) but are safe from fear (21:9). Their cattle breed without fail (a blessing from God, Deut. 28:4, 18). Their little ones dance and play in the street, which is a sign of peace and prosperity (Zech. 8:5). They (the wicked) sing the latest "pop" songs (21:12; Isa. 5:12; Amos 6:5). They live out their days in luxury and die suddenly, without suffering through a long, painful, and expensive illness (21:13; compare Ps. 73:3–5).

Goodbye, God! (21:14–16)

Job argued here that he was not among the cynical, skeptical, practical atheists who brazenly tell God to get lost because they do not need him any longer in order to prosper.

Such people think that they are solely responsible for their prosperity.

> They say to God, "Depart from us!
> We do not desire the knowledge of thy ways.
> What is the Almighty, that we should serve him?
> And what profit do we get if we pray to him?"
> Behold, is not their prosperity in their hand?
> —21:14–16

This type of scepticism on the part of the wicked is reflected in other parts of the Old Testament. Psalm 73:8–9, 11 pictures rich skeptics who "set their mouths against the heavens, and their tongue struts through the earth." Malachi spoke of some in his day who were saying: "It is vain to serve God. What is the good of our keeping his charge or of walking as in mourning before the Lord of hosts? Henceforth, we deem the arrogant blessed; evildoers not only prosper but when they put God to the test they escape." (See Mal. 3:14–15. Also see Isa. 5:18–21.)

But Job was not one of these wicked skeptics. He had not told God to leave. Instead he had asked God repeatedly for an opportunity to come before him. Job was not serving God to gain prosperity: "The council of the wicked" was far from him (21:16).

How Often Is the Lamp of the Wicked Put Out? (21:17–21)

In this section Job went back to the previous speech of Bildad who had asserted that the lamp of the wicked is put out (18:6) and that calamity comes upon them (18:12). Here Job asked, "How often does this happen?" Job did not say that it never happens, but he implied that the wicked often prosper without any obvious suffering or punishment (21:17). He said that the wicked are not always like straw or chaff which the wind drives away, as the wise man asserted in Psalm 1:4.

The friends seem to agree that some wicked men escape punishment; but if they do, it always falls on their children. Job said that if this is true, God is not just; because every man should bear his own guilt and suffer for his own sins (21:19–21). There was in ancient Israel the assertion that the sins of the fathers are visited on their children to the third and fourth generation (Ex. 20:5; 34:7). But in a later time men saw that although there is truth in such a concept, it is basically true that "the fathers shall not be put to death for the children, nor the children be put to death for the fathers; every man shall be put to death for his own sin" (Deut. 24:16; see Jer. 31:29; Ezek. 18:2–4).

There Is No Difference (21:22–26)

Job asserted that there is no difference in the way God treats the wicked and the righteous. The wicked often die in full prosperity, and the righteous often suffer untold misery, never having tasted of the good. They lie down in the dust alike, and worms cover them. Seeing these inequities, one may have been prone to think that God needed to be taught a lesson (21:22), but that is impossible because of his sovereignty. He is so great that he judges the angels, "those that are on high." Therefore, it would be the height of presumptuousness for Job or his friends to attempt to teach God anything.

Job's Friends Are Schemers, Recluses, and Liars (21:27–33)

Perhaps Job had suspected the motives of his friends before, but now he verbalized his thoughts. He accused them of scheming against him.

> Behold, I know your thoughts,
> and your schemes to wrong me.
>
> —21:27

In verses 29–30 Job said that anybody who had been anywhere would know "that the wicked man is spared in the day of calamity" and "is rescued in the day of wrath." No one confronts the wicked with his deeds or calls him to account for what he has done (21:31). He dies and has a big funeral; a guard is placed at his tomb; the clods are sweet to him; and those who file by his bier or make pilgrimages to his tomb are innumerable (21:32–33). In the last verse Job said that his comforters had given him empty nothings and their answers were lies (21:34).

We have come to the end of the second argument. Who won, Job or his friends? Do the wicked always suffer and the righteous always prosper? The answer is, neither Job nor his friends won. There is some truth on both sides, but neither side nor sides have all of the truth. The full explanation remains a mystery. Sometimes the righteous suffer severely. It is not always the most wicked soldiers who get killed in war.

The writer of Ecclesiastes reflected upon the problems of the righteous and the wicked and came to the conclusion that God is vastly indifferent to all that goes on in the world (Eccl. 9:1–3). But what Ecclesiastes called indifference, Jesus called magnanimity. He said, "[God] makes his sun rise on the evil and on the good, and sends rain on the just and on the unjust" (Matt. 5:45). The book of Job does not resolve the problem of why the righteous sometimes suffer, but any answer must be seen in the relationship which Job had with God, not in his relationship to the evidences of his world.

---

1. Terrien, *Interpreter's Bible*, Vol. III, p. 1026.
2. Scherer, *op. cit.*, p. 1026.
3. *Anchor Bible*, Vol. XV, p. 124.
4. Terrien, *Job: Poet of Existance*, p. 145.
5. James Wood, *op. cit.*, p. 77.
6. Balmer H. Kelley, *The Layman's Bible Commentary*, (Richmond, Va.: John Knox Press, 1962), p. 103. Used by permission.
7. T. H. Robinson, *op. cit.*, p. 104.
8. Sherer, *op. cit.*, p. 1059.

6

The Third Argument:

The Sinfulness of Job

(22:1 to 27:23)

THIS THIRD CYCLE of speeches is shorter than the other two. There are 299 verses in the first cycle, 186 verses in the second, and 115 verses in the third cycle. Perhaps this cycle is shorter because the participants (and readers) were getting tired and bored. Perhaps the writer wanted to make the friends' arguments appear boring. Bildad speaks very briefly, and Zophar does not speak at all. This may be because the poet wanted to imply that the friends had been defeated.

This part of Job contains some stimulating thoughts and beautiful expressions such as these:

> Can a man be profitable to God? —22:2

> Is it any pleasure to the Almighty if you are righteous?
> —22:3

> He stretches out the north over the void,
> and hangs the earth upon nothing. —26:7

> Lo, these are but the outskirts of his ways;
> and how small a whisper do we hear of him!
> But the thunder of his power who can understand?
> —26:14

However this section of the book of Job presents special problems to the reader. One writer has entitled his discussion on this section "Confusion." The introductory phrase, "And Job again took up his discourse, and said" (27:1), is repeated in 29:1, seemingly for no reason. Job's speech on the fate of the wicked (27:7–23) sounds very much like what Zophar had been saying about the wicked and the very opposite of what Job had said in chapter 21.

A new style of writing appears in chapter 24. It contains at least eight three-line stanzas (v. 12, 13, 14, 15, 16, 18, 20, 24), and many of the verses do not seem to follow each other logically. Some of the newer translations have taken great liberty in rearranging the verses in this chapter and those surrounding it. Moffatt, for example, placed verse 9 after verse 3; 30:2–8 after 24:8; 24:12 after 24:14; 26:2–4 after 25:1. The New English Bible places 24:6 after 24:2 and 24:9 after 24:3. The Jerusalem Bible transfers 24:18–24 to the end of chapter 27. Norman Snaith placed a chart at the end of his little book on Job showing how twenty-four different scholars have reassigned the various chapters and verses to different speakers.

Eliphaz' Last Words (22:1–30)

"Can a Man Be Profitable to God?" (22:1–5)

Without fanfare or his usual courtesies, Eliphaz plunged into his charges against Job. Job had said (21:27) that he knew about the friends' thoughts and schemes to wrong him. Now the matter was out in the open. All along the friends probably had suspected Job of being a sinner, but had not brought any specific charges against him—except perhaps Zophar's charge that he had crushed and abandoned the poor, and had seized a house which he did not build (20:19). Now Eliphaz listed a whole catalog of Job's sins (22:6–9). But before he did so, he cleared God of any responsibility in Job's suffering. Eliphaz argued that God does not profit or derive any pleasure from the righteousness of men. (22:1–3). God does not stand to gain or lose by man's service to him or by the loss of such service. Job was to serve God without thought of reward, since God does not deal with man on the basis of a hope for personal gain.

Eliphaz' claim is a half-truth. God is no respecter of persons; it would be equally as bad for God to serve man out of a selfish motive as it would be for a man to serve God for such reason. But God is no cold, passionless automaton. He is a loving, compassionate Father. Consider this passage:

> How can I give you up, O Ephraim!
> How can I hand you over, O Israel!
> How can I make you like Admah!
> How can I treat you like Zeboiim!
> My heart recoils within me,
> My compassion grows warm and tender.
> —Hosea 11:8

In 22:4 Eliphaz sarcastically remarked that Job did not get into the condition he was in by going to church, so to speak. It was not because of Job's fear (worship) of God that God had entered into judgment with him. Since God was not responsible for Job's sufferings, they must be due to Job's own sins.

Job's Sins and Their Consequences (22:6–11)

Eliphaz sincerely believed that God could not be responsible for man's suffering; therefore, Job's sufferings had to be due to his sins. So Eliphaz struck out with his imagination, charging Job of sins for which there was no evidence.

When a list of Job's sins was drawn up, it consisted of sins which the rich and powerful often commit—sins of commission and omission against the poor. Job was accused of having taken a pledge from a brother unjustly (22:6); of giving no water or bread to the hungry and thirsty (22:7); of snatching lands away from the needy (22:8); and of not helping widows and orphans (22:9). For Eliphaz, these sins had to be the explanation of Job's suffering. Job specifically denied these sins in chapter 31.

Snares were round about Job, and sudden terrors overwhelmed him (22:10). Darkness came over him and a flood of waters (symbolic of evil) covered him (22:11). And all of this was because of Job's sins.

Misunderstanding of God's Transcendence (22:12–20)

The transcendence of God is a theme which Eliphaz had stressed in all three of his speeches (4:18; 5:9; 15:15). Job also had acknowledged God's transcendence (9:5–10), but Eliphaz believed that Job had drawn the wrong deduction from this concept. God's transcendence does not mean that God is so far removed from the world and man that he cannot see what man is doing. But this is what Eliphaz understood Job to believe about God (22:12–14).

Eliphaz accused Job of following the same course as the men in the days of the Flood (22:16) and the men in the days of Sodom and Gomorrah (22:20). Eliphaz portrayed those ancient sinners as speaking the same words that Job used in 21:14. They did not know that it was God who filled their houses with good things. When those sinners were destroyed by flood and fire, the righteous saw it and rejoiced. The innocent laughed them to scorn (22:19) because, according to Eliphaz, such a sight confirmed God's righteous rule of the universe.

Agree with God and Good Will Come to You (22:21–30)

In this passage, Eliphaz turned away from his harshness and pleaded for Job to repent. The only trouble was that Job did not need to repent of the particular sins which Eliphaz thought he had committed. However, Eliphaz' plea is a good description of repentance. He urged Job: "agree with God," "receive instruction from his [God's] mouth, and lay up his words in your heart," "return to the Almighty," "humble yourself," "remove unrighteousness far from your tents," "to abandon his love for riches, and make God his gold" (see 22:21–25).

Eliphaz seems to have been advocating salvation by works. All of the stress was on what Job should do. Nothing was said about God's love, grace, and forgiveness. Also, Eliphaz continued to maintain his doctrine of retribution, that is, Job's suffering was automatically due to his sins. According to the doctrine of Eliphaz, Job would automatically be wealthy again when he repented and was forgiven (22:21, 28).

Then Eliphaz made a statement that has been translated several ways:

> He will deliver *even* him that is not innocent, Yea he shall be delivered through the cleanness of thy hands.
> —22:30, ASV

> He delivers the innocent man; you will be delivered through the cleanness of your hands.
> —RSV

> He shall deliver the island of the innocent: and it is delivered by the pureness of thine hands.
> —KJV

These are only a few of the variety of translations. And the cause of the disagreement is a small Hebrew particle that can make a word negative, or in some contexts can be translated "island." Either translation provides problems. If you accept the ASV, Eliphaz was saying that men who are not righteous can be made so through Job's prayers. That is, the righteousness of one man can be used to plead for the deliverance of an unclean man.

Later, Job did pray for his friends (see 42:9). Balmer Kelly said concerning 22:30:

> Eliphaz' parting promise is pathetic . . . He has no other solution to offer, although this one is mockery. It stands at odds with the whole biblical message, for deliverance is never on the grounds of man's innocency or the cleanness of his hands but always on the basis of the grace of God.[1]

Any one of the translations leads one to mistrust Eliphaz' theology—a salvation by works that completeley ignored the necessity of God's forgiveness. He not only was a miserable comforter, he was a bad interpreter of God.

These are the last words of Eliphaz. There is something sad about this good man, who tried to help his friend but did not know how. He was so sure of his own position that he was unable to progress into new truths which God was revealing to Job.

Job's Response to Eliphaz (23:1 to 24:25)

Oh, That I Knew Where I Might Find Him (23:1–9)

Eliphaz had admonished Job to "agree with God" (22:21) and to "lay up words" in his heart (22:22). Job replied, "How can I agree with someone I cannot find?" He said that he had treasured in his bosom the words of God's mouth (23:12). God was still hidden to Job. He said, "I go forward, but he is not there" (23:8); "I cannot perceive him" (23:8); "I cannot behold him" (23:9); "I cannot see him" (23:9).

Is not this the experience of every child of God at some time? Are your prayers always answered immediately? An awareness of God may not always be available to man. "Truly thou art a God who hidest thyself" (Isa. 45:15). The prophet said:

> Seek the Lord while he may be found,
> call upon him while he is near.
>
> —Isaiah 55:6

The anguish of verse 3 is the cry of Everyman when he gropes for God in his despair and loneliness. The hiddenness of God—or his seeming unavailability—was a major factor in Job's frustration. One expositor (Scherer) has suggested that God's hiddenness is often the result of our looking for a God who does not exist. "The God Job was looking for was the God of the faith that was dying; in the death of that faith the God of the new faith was revealing himself." [2]

It may be that Job could not find God because he was looking for him in the wrong place or with the wrong attitude. Job seems to have been looking for God in the created universe (23:8–9). God is not to be identified only through his creation. The fullest revelation of God has come through history and not through nature. Man's knowledge of God depends on revelation and not discovery. Man does not have access to any technique by which God can be summoned and compelled to appear. If that were true, God would not be God.

We need not be terrified by the hiddenness of God, for there is another side to the coin. While God hides himself when we look for the wrong thing in the wrong way, he is all the while seeking man, revealing himself in a thousand ways. In Christ, the search for God is completed. In his Son, the God who hides himself revealed himself clearly, unmistakably.

God Sees and Knows Job and Continues to Terrify Him (23:10–17)

Eliphaz had accused Job of saying with the ancient sinners that God could not see man when he sinned (22:14). But Job was aware all along that God could see him (10:4–7), even though he could not see God. Once again Job asserted his innocence and his compliance with the commandments of God (23:11–12). But God had decided, "Is in one mind" (KJV), (not "is unchangeable," as RSV), and no one can turn him away from his course (23:13). Job said that God had purposed many such things for other people as he had for Job (23:14). Therefore Job was terrified. The meaning of 23:17 is debated. Again, the question concerns the presence of a negative particle or Hebrew character, and again it is probably best to retain the negative (against the RSV) and read as follows (author's translation):

> For I am not cut off because of darkness,
> nor because of the shadow that covers my face.
>
> —Job 23:17

Job seems to have been saying that it was not the darkness of suffering that troubled him so much as it was the fact that God brought it on him and he could not see God. He was, he felt, being troubled from a source that he could not see or understand.

Why Does God Allow Sin to Go Unpunished? (24:1–12)

Job turned from his own helpless search for God and elaborated on the thought he had expressed in 23:14, "and many such things are in his [God's] mind." Job saw that what was happening to him was happening to many other helpless people of earth. He asked (24:1) why God does not have a judgment day and right the wrongs that are being done to those who know him. Then Job listed the sins of the wicked against the poor peasants of the land. They removed landmarks and seized flocks and pastured them (24:2). They drove away the ass of the orphan and took the widow's ox for a pledge (24:3). They "thrust the poor off the road" and forced them to hide in caves (24:4). They snatched fatherless children from their mothers and took the infant of the poor in pledge (24:9).

The plight of these poverty stricken people is further described in 24:5–8, 10–11. They had to rustle food for themselves and their children like wild animals (24:5–6). They slept naked because their oppressors had taken their covering in pledge illegally (24:7). They were wet with rain for they did not have adequate shelter (24:8). Unclothed, they worked among the sheaves of the wicked but were not allowed to eat any grain (24:10). They trampled out the wine from the grapes but themselves suffered thirst (24:11). All of this was going on in a supposedly moral universe ruled by a good God. Yet it seemed to Job that "God pays no attention to their prayers" (24:12). That was Job's problem. It was Habakkuk's problem (Hab. 1:2–4, 13), and it is a problem for many today. But Job, like many of us, was better at asking questions than he was in answering them. There are no answers in this passage, only questions.

Those Who Rebel Against the Light (24:13–17)

From the wicked who oppressed the poor, Job turned his attention to those who rebel against the light. Light probably refers both to God and the daylight. Job named three kinds of sinners who operate under the cover of darkness: the murderer, the thief, and the adulterer (24:14–15). Of course, all three of these classes of sinners are more brazen today. Murders, thefts, and acts of adultery are not confined to the night anymore.

What Is Going to Happen to Such Sinners? (24:18–25)

This is a very difficult passage to interpret, as a comparison of the various translations and commentaries will verify. One difficulty is that verses 18–20 say exactly what Job's "friends" had been saying about the wicked and the very opposite of what Job had been saying. Are we to understand that Job suddenly shifted sides without any explanation? Or should we use the device of inserting the words, "You say" at the beginning of verse 18 with the RSV and the margin of the ASV, although the Hebrew text does not have them?

Some students think this section is misplaced and should be put at the end of chapter 27 and counted as a part of Zophar's missing speech.

Kelly expressed another interpretation of this difficult passage:

> It is possible that some timid editor, feeling that Job's words have gone too far in the direction of blasphemy, consequently modified them by inserting this opposite view, using words which in the original form of the book belonged to one of the friends. In so doing he attributed to Job a view which actually negates what Job has just said . . . If this is true, then "You say" in verse 18 should be omitted from the English translation. Verses 22 and 23, moreover, would then be understood as an admission that while God *seems* to give security to the wicked, it is in reality only ephemeral and before long the wicked are carried off like a dry weed or like the head of grain cut from the stalk.[3]

In my view, however, it is probably best to follow the reading in the Revised Standard Version.

In 24:18–20, Job quoted the friends as saying that the wicked would be cut off quickly and finally. But in 24:21–24, he said that God prolongs the life of the wicked. They rise up from serious illnesses. He gives them security and support, and watches over their ways. After reaching a ripe old age, they die quickly without pain. In 24:25 Job challenged his hearers to prove him a liar if there were no truth in what he was saying.

Bildad's Last Words (25:1–6)

Bildad made no attempt to disprove Job's claim that God allows sins to go unpunished. He simply repeated the theological clichés he and Eliphaz had used before. God is sovereign. In heaven there is peace (25:2). Thousands do his bidding and his light shines over all (25:3). How can Job, who is born of woman and is a worm, be righteous before God if the heavenly bodies are not spotless before him (25:4–6)?

Job's Third Speech (26:1–14)

Job's Sarcastic Reply to Bildad (26:1–4)

With biting sarcasm, Job commented on the "wonderful" help his friends had given him in his weakness (26:1). They had counseled him who in their opinion had no wisdom (26:3, compare 12:3; 13:2). They had declared knowledge in profusion (26:3). Then Job asked sarcastically where Bildad got all his strength, wisdom, and knowledge. The implication is that he got it from Eliphaz, who had used the same arguments before (4:17; 15:14). Or, Job may have been implying that Bildad was inspired by an evil spirit (26:4).

Further Acknowledgement of the Greatness of God (26:5–14)

Because Bildad's last speech was so short (25:1–6), and since the ideas expressed in this passage (26:5–14) fit Bildad's repeated emphasis on divine transcendence, many scholars believe this passage is Bildad's speech rather than Job's. It is true that Job also had repeatedly recognized the greatness of God (9:5–10; 12:13–25.) But heretofore when Job had commented on the greatness of God he had always emphasized the negative aspects of God's power. However, a change came over Job (19:25). It is altogether possible therefore, that this passage (26:5–14) is Job's positive evaluation of God's control over Sheol, the earth, and the heavens.

The evaluation of this problem by Andrew Blackwood, Jr., is a very good one. He said: "There is no conclusive argument one way or the other, whether this song of God's infinite power was sung by Bildad or by Job in the first edition. As it stands today, the song in all its wondrous beauty is Job's. Whoever first sang it, to me it is the most beautiful section in the book." [4]

In 26:5–6 Job said that the "shades" (the dead who are only shadows of their former selves) tremble along with the subterranean waters (symbols of evil) and their inhabitants. Sheol and Abaddon are subject to God. "Abaddon" is from the Hebrew word *'bd* meaning destruction. Some passages in the Old Testament may seem to imply that God consequently has no power over it. (Compare Ps. 6:5; 30:9; 88:10–12; 115:17; Isa. 38:18.) But in Job 26:5–6 and in Psalm 139:8 God's sovereignty is understood as controlling Sheol.

God stretches out the north (Zaphon—the mountain of the gods) over the void (*tohu*), and hangs the earth upon nothing (26:7). By his reference to "the north," the writer is probably claiming God's sovereignty over all would-be gods. He made the place where they dwell. The references to "void" and "nothing" reflect what came to be the basis for the doctrine of creation—*ex nihilo,* "out of nothing." We should not understand that the speaker is describing the earth as a ball hung in space. He is describing the earth as flat and solid but as receiving its support and stability from the Creator God (26:7).

Verse 8 describes the miracle of the flimsy clouds heavy with water yet not breaking. God covers the face of his throne (not "moon" as RSV and NEB) and spreads a cloud over it (26:9). He has drawn a circle as the horizon which separates the light and darkness. But this circle probably is intended as a boundary to keep in check the powers of chaos, represented by the waters (26:10). The language here reflects the writer's acquaintance with some of the accounts of creation produced by Israel's neighbors. The inspired writer of Job used this old language to proclaim God's sovereignty over all cosmic powers:

> By his power he stilled the sea; by his understanding he smote Rahab. By his wind the heavens were made fair; his hand pierced the fleeing serpent.
>
> —26:12–13, RSV

> He divideth the sea with his power, and by his understanding he smiteth through the proud. By his Spirit he hath garnished the heavens; his hand hath formed the crooked serpent.
>
> —26:12–13, KJV

(Note the use of Rahab for "proud" For other uses of the term see Job 9:13; Isa. 51:9; and Ps. 89:10.)

Like the writer of Psalm 8, who marveled at the greatness of God when he saw the heavens the work of God's fingers (Ps. 8:3), the speaker in 26:14 exclaimed that these marvelous manifestations of God in creation represent only "the outskirts of his ways."

> Lo, these are but the outskirts of his ways;
> and how small a whisper do we hear of him!
> But the thunder of his power who can understand?

"These" refers to creation and the natural world, from which man can get some idea of God's power and greatness, but they cannot furnish man with a full revelation. They are only the "outskirts of his ways" and a mere whisper. Where can man find out more about God? The passage seems to imply that man cannot understand much more than that: "But the thunder of his power who can understand?" We know that the creation of the universe was a marvelous feat, but God does not reveal his love and grace primarily through nature. It is only in history, and supremely in the cross, that God reveals his love.

Job Speaks Again (27:1–23)

Job Maintains His Innocence (27:1–7)

There is little doubt that Job is speaking in this section. We might have expected a third speech from Zophar after Job's third speech, but as the text stands Zophar did not appear again. Does that mean that Zophar admitted defeat? Perhaps so, but that is not like Zophar.

Some scholars believe that 27:7–23 or 27:13–23 is Zophar's third speech. It must be admitted that these verses sound like Zophar's previous speeches on the fate of the wicked. But there is no manuscript evidence to support such a theory. Therefore, we must try to understand this chapter as the speech of Job.

Chapter 27:1 is repeated in 29:1 as an introduction to

Job's further remarks. In 27:2 Job swore ("As God lives") by the very God who, he said, had taken away his right and left his soul bitter. Job swore that as long as he lived (which depended on the Spirit of God) he would not speak falsehood or utter deceit. He would not lie even for God, as he accused his friends of doing (13:7). He would not say he had sinned when he had not. He would maintain his integrity. His conscience was clear (27:6).

Job, the Righteous; His Enemy, the Wicked (27:7–12)

Job had just declared his righteousness; that is, he asserted that he had maintained his part of the covenant with God. Therefore, if Job was righteous, his enemy must be wicked (27:7). His friends had been holding out a hope for him. Job said that if he were as ungodly as his friends had claimed, he had no hope, for the ungodly are without hope (27:8). God takes away the life of the ungodly man and will not hear his prayers. If Job were ungodly, it would do him no good to pray as his friends had admonished him to do (5:8; 8:5; 11:13).

Now Job said in effect: I will teach you concerning the hand [power, NEB] of God (27:11). You [friends] have been trying to teach me about God's power. All of you have seen it; why have you become altogether empty? (See 27:12.)

What was it that Job was going to teach his friends and not conceal any longer? Was it the speech that follows—one about the fate of the wicked—that sounds so much like what Zophar has already said? If so, Job would be teaching them nothing new, unless Job was saying in effect: You are the wicked ones, and what you said would happen to me is really going to happen to you. You are the wicked ones; not I.

Some scholars think that what Job was going to teach his friends about the hand of God is to be found in chapter 28. That chapter teaches that God's ways are mysterious, and true wisdom is found only in God. But Job's friends had already acknowledged both those truths (11:7).

The speaker in 27:13–23 gave us a classic statement of the retributive view of suffering and the fate of the wicked, which the friends have maintained all along. The retributive or penal view is true in some cases. It certainly was not true in Job's case.

1. Kelly, *op. cit.*, p. 109.
2. Scherer, *op. cit.*, p. 1080.
3. Kelly, *op. cit.*, p. 113.
4. Andrew W. Blackwood, Jr., *Devotional Introduction to Job* (Grand Rapids: Baker Book House, 1952), p. 111. Used by permission.

7

A Musical Interlude:
A Hymn in Praise of Wisdom

(28:1–28)

A DELIGHTFUL and welcome change in mood and movement of the book of Job takes place in chapter 28. By this time the main characters, as well as the readers of the book, have grown weary. Many modern readers never get this far. Chapter 28 represents a break in the action of dialogue. It corresponds to the role of the chorus in a Greek tragedy and serves to slow down the argument. It is like the application of the foot brake on an automobile or the deployment of the parachute on a returning space vehicle. Chapter 28 is a hymn in praise of wisdom, both man's and God's.

Does this chapter fit into the scheme of the book of Job? It seems to have little relationship to that which precedes or follows it. It cannot be positively attributed to Job or any one of his friends. Many modern scholars believe that it is a later addition to the book of Job, either by the original author or by a different writer. Some interpreters hold that the poem is authentic except for the last verse (28). Others ably defend this chapter as the work of the original author and see no reason for denying the last verse to the writer. In fact, say some, the whole point of the poem is in the last verse. The prose introduction to 28:28, "And he said to man" clearly sets it off from the rest of the poem as if to say, "This is the conclusion of the whole matter."

> Behold, the fear of the Lord, that is wisdom;
> and to depart from evil is understanding.
>
> —28:28

One is reminded by this verse of the statement made about Job three times in the prologue. Job is described as "one who feared God and turned away from evil" (1:1, 8; 2:3). Job was a wise man, and those who came to counsel him were left in silence.

This chapter furnishes one answer to Job's problem of why God allowed him to suffer, why God did not answer him when he could not comprehend the ways of the Almighty. The answer is that man cannot attain that kind of knowledge. Wisdom like that is found only in God. But man should rightly relate himself to God ("fear him") and turn away from evil. The hymn can be divided into three parts: man cannot find wisdom through technology (28:1–11); man cannot get wisdom through manipulation or money (28:12–19); wisdom which is hidden from the living and the dead is only attainable from God, since he is the Creator and Ruler of the world (28:20–28).

Man Cannot Find Wisdom Through Technology (28:1–11)

Technology was very primitive in many respects in the ancient world. The stage of technology in that day can be seen most clearly, perhaps, in buildings and mining. This section of Job is one of the few places in the Bible where mining is mentioned. The author of this passage must have had first-hand knowledge of some kind of mine. He referred to mines for gold, silver, iron, and copper.

There were silver mines in Tarshish (probably in Spain) and gold mines in Nubia. Iron was mined in northern Palestine, and ancient copper mines have been found in the Negeb and the Sinai Peninsula. Man had been able to accomplish some amazing feats in mining. He had been able to open deep shafts in the bosom of the earth, drive back the deep darkness with lights, descend and ascend by ropes, and take out of the earth ore, precious stones, and dust of gold (28:1–6).

Man had gone where a beast had never been or where the eye of a bird had never seen (28:7–8). Some scholars think that the subject of verses 7 and 8 is wisdom. If that is true then the writer is saying that the eye of a bird has never seen wisdom, and no beast has trodden the path to wisdom. Man may be able to overturn mountains, cut channels in rocks, dam up huge rivers, and bring to light that which is hidden, but he cannot find wisdom through technology.

Man's achievements in science are to be applauded. This fact is true of our age more than any other. But science has not solved all of modern man's problems, and it cannot do so. Since time immemorial man has been engaged in a continuous struggle with the natural world, and man has gained the mastery over much of it. But while he pursues the conquest of space, he pollutes his environment and fails to control his spirit.

Man Cannot Find Wisdom Through Manipulation or Money (28:12–19)

If wisdom cannot be found through technology, perhaps it can be obtained in some other way. This section of Job also sounds modern. Some men think that a way can be found to get anything one desires. If it cannot be mined or manufactured, it can be obtained either by manipulation or by money. Ours is the age of the manipulators. Men in politics know how to manipulate news, laws, and voters. Businessmen and industrialists know how to manipulate prices, stocks, bonds, taxes, and workers. Labor leaders know how to manipulate man-hours and wages. Some church leaders have been accused of trying to manipulate their congregations, and some Christians may be guilty of trying to manipulate the Lord.

The question is asked in 28:12 and again in 28:20: "Where shall wisdom be found, and where is the place of understanding?" The deep and the sea reply, "It is not in me." The "deep" and "sea" are personified here as they are elsewhere in the Old Testament (see 7:12). The assertion is made that wisdom cannot be found by trying to manipulate the supposedly primeval powers of the sea or death (28:22).

If wisdom is unattainable by technology and by manipulation, it is also unavailable through money. Some people seem to think that money can buy anything and everything. But wisdom is not for sale.

> It [wisdom] cannot be gotten for gold,
>   and silver cannot be weighed as its price.
> It cannot be valued in the gold of Ophir,
>   in precious onyx or sapphire.
> Gold and glass cannot equal it
>   nor can it be exchanged for jewels of fine gold.
> No mention shall be made of coral or of crystal;
>   the price of wisdom is above pearls.
> The topaz of Ethiopia cannot compare with it,
>   nor can it be valued in pure gold.
>
> —28:15–19

Men may know how to mine silver, gold, and precious stones. Valuable and rare as these things are, they cannot be exchanged for wisdom. Wisdom is a different kind of commodity. It is like love, faithfulness, and goodness. It is something that each man must obtain for himself through the grace of God.

Only God the Creator Knows the Place of Wisdom (28:21–28)

Earlier Job asked, "Who can understand the thunder of his power?" (26:14). In 28:23 we read: "God understands." God understands the dwelling place of wisdom. He knows its place, for he can see everything under the heavens (28:23–24). This God who knows the dwelling place of wisdom "gave to the wind its weight" (its velocity) and measured out the waters of the sea. He made "a decree for the rain," assigning the place and the amount of it; he assigned the path of thunder and lightning (28:25–26). God created and operates the natural world, and he did it (and continues to do it) with wisdom.

> Then he saw it [wisdom] and declared it;
>   he established it, and searched it out.
>
> —28:27

God is wise. His wisdom is demonstrated in his creation and control of the universe. Man cannot know all that God knows because man is limited. Man cannot see all there is to see, but God can (28:24). Man is limited in power. Only God can create and control a universe. There is, then, a type and a dimension of wisdom which belongs only to God.

Is there a truth here for us today? There is a boundary line or frontier beyond which the mind of man cannot see. There is a limit to man's power and skill. Man can learn many things and can harness the basic energy of the universe. But he cannot find ultimate wisdom through science. Man's conquest of nature should not fool him. His behavior betrays him; his power corrupts him. Man's wisdom consists in fearing God and turning away from evil (28:28).

8

Job's Summary of His Case

(29:1 to 31:40)

WITH the close of the musical interlude (chap. 28), we turn our attention back to center stage and find Job all alone. Perhaps his three friends were still in the background, but in this section Job was not speaking primarily to them. Indirectly he may have been speaking to God. But for the most part he was speaking to himself. He was pouring out his soul; he was verbalizing his innermost thoughts (30:16).

Job's summary consists of three main parts: his past, 29:1–25; his present, 30:1–31; and his oath of innocence and challenge of God, 31:1–40.

Job's Past (29:1–25)

It is natural for people on a journey to stop occasionally for a look back to where they have been. There is nothing wrong in that, as long as one does not want to return to the past and live there forever. Job had a healthy approach to the past. He knew he could not "go home again." We have heard nothing of Job's previous happy days since chapter 1. So it is not too much to expect a backward glance at the life that Job had lived in earlier days. We should be thankful for this fuller statement of what Job's life was like before tragedy came.

"In those days," Job said, "God watched over me; . . . his

lamp shone upon my head, and by his light I walked" (29: 1–3). The expression "autumn days" in verse 4 refers to the season of harvest, which symbolizes maturity and prosperity, rather than to the closing days of one's life. Job speaks of the friendship and the presence of God during those early days. It was a time when his children were about him, and his "steps were washed with milk" ("butter," KJV, 29:5–6). It was a time when he was respected in the community. Old and young alike arose when he came near. Princes and noblemen stopped talking as he approached (29:7–10).

The picture here seems to be of Job as a king, since princes and noblemen would show respect only to their superiors. He is presented in 1:3 as "the greatest of all the people [the sons] of the East." If Job had been a king, that fact would explain the reference to his delivering the poor, the fatherless, and widows in 29:12–13, since that was the responsibility of the king (Ps. 72:2, 4, 12–14).

Eliphaz had accused Job of not giving bread to the hungry, of withholding water from the weary, and of sending widows and orphans away empty (22:7, 9). Job specifically denied these charges (29:12–13).

When Job said, "I put on righteousness" (29:14) he was making no claim of self-righteousness. He was simply stating that he was fulfilling his covenant obligations to God and man.

What a tremendous assertion Job made when he said, "I was eyes to the blind and feet to the lame" (29:15). He claimed that he helped men see who could not see otherwise, and he helped them achieve what they could not have achieved alone. Vision and power for others was the work of Job previously. In those days, Job had assumed that things would be the same forever. He would "multiply his days as the sand and die in his nest," but such was not to be.

Job's Present (30:1–31)

From discussing those glorious days of the past, Job turned to the wretchedness of the present. Just as he did not magnify his material blessing, so here he did not dwell morbidly on his physical sufferings. One of the hardest things for Job to accept in his experience of suffering was the loss of the respect of the people around him. Evidently, though, it had been a superficial respect, based only on his position, power, wealth, and prestige. When he lost those things, he lost the homage that went with them.

Having been treated like a king, Job could not get used to being treated like an outcast, even when he was being made an outcast for God's sake. Is not becoming an outcast for God's sake precisely what the suffering servant of Isaiah 53 did willingly? Is this not what Jesus did? Paul said of Jesus: "Who, though he was in the form of God, did not count equality with God a thing to be grasped, but emptied himself, taking the form of a servant" (Phil. 2:6–7). Job could not do that! He lamented the fact that the youth of the lowest stratum of society made sport of him. The ignorant, disreputable brood who lived in communes, in gullies and caves abhorred him, made him a byword, and spat at the sight of him (30:1-10).

One last time, Job blamed God for all of his troubles. He called God a cruel God (30:21) and said that God had cast him into the mire, tossed him about in the roar of a storm, and was bringing him to the point of death, "the house appointed for all living" (30:11, 19–23).

Almost like a spoiled child, Job complained that his neighbors should not have abandoned him. He, himself, had wept for those whose day was hard, and his soul had grieved for the poor (30:25). Now no one wept for him. All of Job's hopes had been dashed to pieces; his light turned to darkness (30:26). He cried for help, but no one responded (30:28–29). His insides were in constant turmoil (30:27) ; pain constantly racked his body (30:17) ; his skin had turned black and fallen from him; and his funeral songs were already arranged (30:28, 30–31).

Job's Oath of Innocence (31:1–40)

It has been said that chapter 31 of Job "reflects a standard of behavior which is unexcelled either in the Old Testament, the literature of the Ancient Near East and classical Greece, or in the New Testament, not excluding the Sermon on the

Mount."[1] This passage is great not only because of the exhaustive list of the sins of which Job claimed to be innocent, but also because of his awareness that sins begin in the heart (31:1, 7, 9, 27, 33). Furthermore, this chapter reflects "a refinement of social thoughtfulness and generosity which is quite unique in the history of ethics."[2]

The form of this chapter is interesting. It is made up of a series of oaths, called oaths of innocence. Each oath begins with "if" and moves on to a "then." There was in ancient Israel the custom, or law, that required anyone who claimed to be innocent when he was accused of a crime to go to the sanctuary and take the oath of innocence (see Num. 5:11–22; Ex. 22:10–11; 1 Kings 8:31–32; Ps. 7:3–5). This chapter shows Job as he stood before the Lord, perhaps at a sanctuary, and swore sixteen times that he was innocent of all the charges that he could imagine.

The Lustful Look (31:1–4)

Job dealt first with his innocence of sexual sins. Perhaps then, as today, sexual sins had saturated society. Job's claim no doubt would be called "puritanical" today. He refused to look lustfully on any woman (see Matt. 5:27–28). The wise men of the Old Testament knew the strong allurement of sensuality, but they also knew its destructive and deadly effects (Prov. 5:8–14; 6:24–35; 7:25–27).

Job asked what the effects of the sin of fornication would have been if he had succumbed to its temptation.

> What would be my portion from God above,
> and my heritage from the Almighty on high?
> Does not calamity befall the unrighteous,
> and disaster the workers of iniquity?
>
> —31:2–3

Job implied that there were three things that restrained him from sinning: the thought that sin would cut him off from God (31:2); the fear of punishment or judgment (31:3); and the thought that God's all-seeing eye was upon him (31:4). At that stage of his life Job believed that God would punish him immediately if he sinned.

Lying and Deceit (31:5–8)

Job knew that God did not judge men by their outward appearance or by their conduct alone. God looks on the heart (1 Sam. 16:7; Prov. 4:23). Job swore that he was perfect, whole, blameless and upright within and without.

> If I have walked with falsehood,
> and my foot has hastened to deceit;
> (Let me be weighed in a just balance,
> and let God know my integrity!)
> if my step has turned aside from the way,
> and my heart has gone after my eyes,
> and if any spot has cleaved to my hands;
> then let me sow, and another eat;
> and let what grows for me be rooted out.
> —31:5–8

Job was so confident that he was innocent that he called the curse of God to come down upon him if he were guilty (31:8; compare Lev. 26:16; Deut. 28:30–33).

Adultery (31:9–12)

Some interpreters express surprise and unbelief that Job would deal with sexual sins twice in twelve verses. Many of them emend the text in verse 1, changing "virgin" to "folly" or "calamity." But there is no need to alter the text since sexual offenses are recognized as heinous crimes (31:11; Lev. 18:17; 20:14). Job said that adultery is an iniquity to be punished by both man and God. It is a fire which consumes all that a man has (31:12). The seriousness of this sin would have, in Job's eyes, merited this special mention.

All Men Are Equal (31:13–15)

Here is one of the most amazing passages in the Old Testament. Job disclaimed any doctrine of discrimination based on race or social distinction. "Did not he who made me in the womb make him [manservant]?" T. H. Robinson caught the spirit of this passage when he said:

> There is no room for a doctrine of the inferior being who is a slave by nature. There is no room for social

> distinctions or for racial discrimination. Job has risen to a height far above that of much in our modern world. There are no grades of humanity, whether due to colour, financial standing, nationality, or any other cause. When we stand in view of our infinite Maker, we must all be equally insignificant, and of equal value in His sight. Job has fully recognized this. The mere fact that these people are in subordination to him by common law and custom does not give him the right to ignore their human status. If they think that they have reason to charge their master with wrong doing, he must grant them the same right to a fair hearing that he himself would expect from his equals. He must abandon any privileges which law and custom allow him, and treat the matter impartially. If he is in the wrong, if they can prove their case, then he must admit the fact and make what amends may be in his power.[3]

The wisdom writers of the Old Testament, with their concern for the individual and for the good life, seem to have been the first to conceive the idea that the privileged good life should extend equally to all classes and races (Prov. 14: 31; 17:5, 22:2; Eph. 6:9).[4]

The Disadvantaged (31:16–23)

We are hearing much in our day about the disadvantaged in our society, and we should hear more. Every society in history has had its disadvantaged. The Old Testament constantly speaks of the poor, the fatherless, and widows. Job swore that he had never taken advantage of other people's misfortunes. In fact, he said that he had shared his food and possessions with such people. It is interesting to note that in many places in this chapter Job confessed that one reason for his right conduct was his consciousness of the judgment of God (31:14, 23).

Worship (31:24–28)

Job knew that proper treatment of the disadvantaged was not enough. His first and basic loyalty and devotion must be to God, as the First Commandment required. In this passage Job asserted that though he was rich he never made his gold an idol (31:24–25). Neither did he become a nature worshiper and confuse the thing created with the Creator (31:26–27). To do so would have meant a denial of the true God above and a breaking of his part of the covenant with God.

Generosity, Hospitality, and Sincerity (31:29–34)

It might not be quite accurate to say that Job loved his enemies, but at least he asserted that he did not rejoice when evil came upon those who hated him (31:29). He had not allowed his mouth to sin by asking for the life of his enemy with a curse. Job seems to have been close to the ideal set by Jesus regarding treatment of one's enemies (see Matt. 5:43–48).

Some see Job's statements concerning his enemy as the high-water mark of ethical expression in the Old Testament. One interpreter has said that if chapter 31 is the crown of the whole ethical development in the Old Testament, verse 29 is the jewel of that crown. In reference to 31:30 another has written: "If the writer of Job knew such prayers as 'In Thy loving-kindness destroy all them that afflict my soul' (Ps. 143:12), 'Send out Thine arrows and destroy them' (Ps. 144:6), or such Psalms as 7, 35, 69, 109, he kept his lips closed while others sang them. . . . But his heart would have burned within him if he could have listened to Matt. 5:43–48." [5]

Hospitality was a necessity as well as a requirement in the ancient world (Ex. 22:21; Job 19:15). There were no hotel or motel facilities for travelers. Since travelers might be subject to the worst kind of abuse at night (Gen. 19:2; Judg. 19:20), citizens were required to receive travelers into the security of their homes. Job said that the sojourner did not need to lodge in the street of his city, because he opened his doors to the wayfarer (31:32). One of the admonitions of Paul to the early Christians was that they be "given to hospitality" (Rom. 12:13, KJV).

In all of his dealings Job had been open and above board. He vowed that he had never been hypocritical, although there might have been reason to be, since he was surrounded by a great multitude of unsympathetic people who had only contempt for him. He had been so terrified that he was afraid to go outdoors (31:33–34). The text seems to break off at the end of verse 34. Some scholars think that Job's thought turned so abruptly from his oath of innocence to his final challenge before God that he did not even finish his sentence.

Job's Final Challenge to God (31:35–37)

Was Job just being an egotist when he spoke these words? Should man challenge God? Was not this the sin of Adam and Eve (Gen. 3)? Was not this the error of the builders of the Tower of Babel (Gen. 11)? If Job, by his oath of innocence, was trying to force open the lock of heaven, he had made his blamelessness (morality) a tool of self-deification. His very uprightness had become the occasion and the basis of his demand for justification from God. Job's approaching God as a prince, throwing down the gauntlet by affixing his *tau* (signature) to his oath of innocence—this is proof that he was lacking in his "fear of God." Job seems to have been declaring his independence of God or his equality with God. Therein is his fatal flaw. Terrien said that man always loses touch with God when he seeks to be independent within the limits of his existence. The problem of atheism is really the problem of a sort of self-directed humanism.

Chapter 31 would have been a wonderful standard of human conduct if it had not been for Job's challenge of God in verses 35–37. The chapter as it stands now ends on a low note. After Job's audacious challenge of God, one might expect God's immediate reply. Instead, we find one more item of Job's oath of innocence (31:38–40). Many writers transpose these verses to some place earlier in the chapter because the thoughts are anticlimactic at the end of the chapter. But several scholars argue that on a number of occasions the author placed the climax of a speech not at the end of the discourse but just prior to it, so that the emotional pitch returns to normal before the speaker has finished.

At the end of chapter 31 the imaginative reader waits breathlessly for God to speak. What a letdown he experiences when he turns to the next chapter (32) to find prose rather than poetry and the blasts of Elihu rather than the voice of God.

Before we leave Job waiting for God's reply, we should ask ourselves whether or not we have properly judged Job. Have we been too hard on him? Has our criticism of him been on the basis of our Christian doctrine of justification by faith alone? We must not accuse Job of impurity, dishonesty, and insincerity. There is no virtue in calling oneself bad names if they are not deserved. We must not confess sins we have not committed. Job was right in challenging his friends' doctrine of retribution as the only view of suffering. He was right in asking God for answers to some of his questions. But he was wrong in approaching God like a prince or a peacock, demanding to be heard and exonerated.

---

1. Terrien, *Job: Poet of Existence*, p. 186; See T. H. Robinson, *op. cit.*, p. 111; H. W. Robinson, *The Cross in the Old Testament* (Philadelphia: Westminster Press, 1955), p. 30; James Strahan, *The Book of Job* (Edinburgh: T. and T. Clark, 1913), p. 243.
2. Terrien, *op. cit.*, p. 186.
3. T. H. Robinson, *op. cit.*, p. 113; compare Pope, *Job, op. cit.*, p. 204.
4. For a fuller discussion of the problems of race in the Old Testament see Ralph L. Smith, "The Race Issue in the Old Testament," in *The Cutting Edge*, edited by H. C. Brown, Jr. (Waco, Texas: Word Books, 1969), Vol. I, pp. 32-41.
5. Strahan, *op. cit.*, p. 263.

9

Elihu:

An Angry Young Man's Defense of God

(32:1—37:34)

JOB'S OATH of innocence was over; his challenge of God was done. Job's three friends were silent because they were convinced that no man could vanquish Job (32:13). Suddenly an intruder bursts onto the platform. He has not appeared before in the story. He is not mentioned in the prologue, the dialogue, the speeches of Yahweh, or in the epilogue. For this reason, among others, many Old Testament scholars believe that these speeches of Elihu were not a part of the original book of Job. It must be admitted that Elihu's appearance in the book at this juncture is somewhat surprising, because most readers are expecting God himself to appear or at least the voice of God to speak in answer to the charges of Job. Furthermore, Elihu is a new character; he was not mentioned in the prologue.

Regarding arguments against Elihu's speech being a part of the original manuscript, one writer has this to say:

> All of these considerations are in the end matters of taste, and one must be hesitant about imposing standards of taste, especially modern ones, upon the creations of antiquity. One could affirm, with justice, that

> Elihu was not mentioned in the prologue because he was not part of the original story used by the author as dramatic background, but that the author deliberately held him in reserve for dramatic effect, intending to present some of his own theological positions through this new mouth.[1]

Who was Elihu? What was he doing here? What did he say? Was he able to accomplish what Job's three friends could not accomplish; namely, convince Job that he was suffering because he had sinned? Was he able to exonerate God?

A brief geneology is given for Elihu, a fact that is not true in the case of Job or his three friends. The name Elihu means "my God is he," and seems to have been fairly common in ancient Israel (1 Sam. 1:1; 1 Chron. 12:20; 26:7; 27:18). His father's name, Barachel, meaning "blessed of God," is found nowhere else in the Old Testament. It does occur in some old Akkadian documents. Elihu is said to have been a Buzite, which probably means that he was an Aramean or an Arab (Gen. 22:20–21; Jer. 25:23). However, the name of Elihu's family, Ram, is usually connected with the tribe of Judah in the Old Testament (Ruth 4:19; 1 Chron. 2:9, 25, 27).

Elihu was an interested, articulate young man who grew impatient with the older generation's handling of the theological and practical problems of faith. He waited very impatiently until Job's argument with his friends stopped on dead center. Then Elihu jumped into the fray with both feet. He came out of his corner waving his arms, gritting his teeth, ready to take on both sides in the argument.

Four times in five verses (32:1–5) we are told that Elihu became angry. Probably Elihu's anger was partly due to his youth. Young people are often impulsive and impatient. They are often idealistic and revolutionary. They have keen perceptive powers which enable them to detect flaws in the fabric of the present society and in the prevailing theology. But too often they want to discard that which is old and *good,* as well as that which is old and *bad,* and begin all over again from scratch. Such a process in this nuclear age would turn the clock back to the Stone Age.

Elihu was angry with Job "because he justified himself

rather than God" (32:2). Perhaps Job's closing remarks in chapter 31 about approaching God like a prince were too much for Elihu. He was also angry with Job's three friends—they were not Elihu's friends—because of their bungling incompetence in arguing with Job (32:3–5). Elihu's aim was to rebuke Job and his friends; to answer Job's questions; and to come to God's aid. Elihu, like Peter the apostle, was impulsive. Elihu was answering Job's challenge to God before God had a chance to say a word. How presumptuous of Elihu to think that God needed to be defended by him.

In the past some scholars have claimed that the book of Job is a theodicy, that is, an attempt to justify the ways of God to man. But if this were true, it is strange that the only people in the book who seem to try that are the three friends and Elihu, and they all fail. Job made no attempt to justify the ways of God. The voice of Yahweh in chapters 38–41 certainly offers no apology for his conduct. The epilogue gives no explanation or defense of God. He can take care of himself. His ways are, indeed, past finding out.

Our generation was made aware of a new challenge to God a few years ago when an international news magazine carried a cover story entitled "God Is Dead." Some pastors and theologians immediately jumped to God's rescue. Now a few years later God seems still to be alive and well, but it is doubtful that God's good health should be attributed to the apologies and aid of modern churchmen. Anthony Towne, author of the piercing satire of the "death of God" theologians, *The Obituary of God,* may have captured God's reaction to the whole controversy when he said that God was "bored with it all." [2]

God's existence does not depend upon man's ability to defend him. He is capable of taking care of himself. This does not mean that men should not be concerned with apologetics. Men should be able to give a reason for the faith that is in them (1 Peter 3:15). But proving God's existence or justifying his ways is not man's responsibility.

Elihu tried to do what his elders were unable to do—convince Job that he was suffering because of his sins. In this he failed more miserably than his predecessors; Job did not even bother to answer any of Elihu's words.

Elihu's speeches are hard to outline because he frequently returned to themes he had already discussed. After a brief poetic apology for speaking (32:6–22), Elihu delivered four addresses to Job and his wise friends. The themes of the four addresses are: God speaks to man, 33:1–33; God is just, 34:1–37; God is not obligated to man, 35:1–16; God is just and great, 36:1 to 37:24.

Elihu's Apology for Speaking (32:1–22)

As we have seen, Elihu is a johnny-come-lately in the book of Job. He arrived on the scene just before the climax of the book. In fact, it appears that he interrupted the natural progress of the story. One would expect God to speak after Job's last challenge. But Elihu, who had been standing on the sidelines, was afraid that Job had won the argument with his three friends. He did not want that to happen. He felt that there was still time to salvage part of the argument.

Elihu explained that, in deference to the age of the participants, he had waited to speak. But now, since the friends were silent, he could contain himself no longer. He asked for a hearing from the disputants on the grounds that wisdom does not always come with age (32:9). Elihu claimed that understanding is a gift of the Spirit of God which is not limited to old age. He claimed to speak impartially, forthrightly, uprightly, sincerely, and in the fear of God (32:21–22; 33:3).

God Speaks to Man (33:1–33)

Elihu addressed himself first to Job and asked Job to present his case (33:5). Because Elihu was a man just like Job, Job should have no need to fear him (33:6–7). Can you imagine such presumptuousness? Job had asked to appear before God. Now a brash young man says, "Stand before me and answer me if you can!" (33:5).

Elihu repeated almost verbatim some of Job's claims, which he intended to refute. In the first place Job had claimed to be clean and pure, without transgression or iniquity (9:21; 10:7; 16:17; 23:10; 27:5; 31:7). Secondly, Job had charged that God counted him as an enemy (13:24; 19:11;

30:21), had put his feet in stocks (13:27), and watched him like a hawk (7:17–20). In the next chapter, Elihu returned to these charges. Here he tried to refute them with one broad generalization:

> Behold, in this you are not right.
> I will answer you.
> God is greater than man. —33:12

Then Elihu took up a third claim which Job had made. Job had said that God would not answer any of his questions or speak to him (33:13; 19:7; 30:20). Now Elihu said that God does speak to men. He speaks to men in dreams and warns them to turn away from their pride in order to keep life from perishing. When Elihu appealed to dreams as a method of communication between God and man, he showed himself a companion of Eliphaz, who used his dream as the basis of all of his speeches (4:12–21).

The second way God speaks to man, according to Elihu, is through suffering. This idea was not new with Elihu. Eliphaz had mentioned the disciplinary view of suffering and God's intention to save the sufferer (5:17–27). But here Elihu elaborated on the theory and applied it specifically to Job's case (33:19–22). He said that sometimes God allows a man to suffer and to be brought into the very presence of the death angel to bring him to repentance (33:22–27).

Elihu seems to have suggested a third way in which God speaks to man. That is, God speaks through a mediator, or an interpreter, who not only declares to man what is right, but who also intercedes for him, saying to the death angel:

> Deliver him from going down to the Pit,
> I have found a ransom. —33:24

Neither the ransom nor the interpreter, or mediator, are identified in this passage (33:23–24). The interpreter seems to be an angel, "one of the thousand." The ransom might be the suffering or the repentance of the sick man. But it is more likely that Elihu understood the ransom to be some type of sacrifice. Here Elihu came close to Job's thought of an umpire and redeemer.

According to this view of suffering, the sick man would be restored to health (33:25) and then would go down to the temple to praise God for his salvation (33:26–28). Elihu said that all of these attempts of God to communicate with man are designed to redeem and justify man (33:29–33).

God Is Just (34:1–37)

Elihu would not allow God's grace to overshadow his justice. In this chapter, the young man vigorously defends the justice of God, but in doing so his theology of suffering necessitated that he condemn Job as a great sinner. Elihu still could not see that a man might be a great sufferer and a great saint at the same time. He thought that God and man cannot both be just. Elihu believed that either Job or God was wicked. It could not be God, therefore it must be Job.

John Paterson traced the development of men's understanding of the relationship of suffering and sin in the Bible. At first the theology of many in Israel said that *all sufferers are sinners*. Then some men concluded from the experiences of Jeremiah and others that *some sufferers are saints*. Finally, a prophet in Isaiah 53 moved on to say *some sufferers are saviors*.[3]

It would seem that Elihu never accepted even the second plateau. He said of Job:

> What man is like Job,
>   who drinks up scoffing like water,
> who goes in company with evildoers
>   and walks with wicked men?
> For he has said, "It profits a man nothing
>   that he should take delight in God." —34:7–9

Elihu gave two reasons why God is just. One is because God is sovereign, or omnipotent (34:10–20). This argument sounds too much like the idea that might makes right. It is not, therefore, a very convincing argument. We should not deny the sovereignty of God, but neither should we use his sovereignty to guarantee his justice. A second reason Elihu gave to justify God is the fact that God is omniscient (34:21–28). Therefore, when this just, omnipotent, and omniscient God is silent, who can condemn him (34:29–30)? Elihu implied that, in justifying himself, Job condemned God. In this respect Elihu came close to what Yahweh himself said in 40:8.

Elihu charged that Job had never been moved by his chastisement but continued to try to dictate to God his terms of forgiveness (34:31–33). Elihu agreed with Job's friends and the voice of God that Job had spoken without knowledge (34:35; see 38:2). Like Zophar (11:4–6), Elihu wished that God would speak to Job and give him what he deserved, for Elihu was convinced that Job was a rebel and a heretic. The reference to Job's handclapping and blasphemies in verse 37 shows that Elihu regarded Job as a "dangerous and incorrigible heretic."

God Is Not Obligated to Man (35:1–16)

Here we return to one of the key issues in the book of Job. The question that Elihu attributes to Job (35:2–3) is almost identical to the one that Satan asked in 1:9, "Does Job fear God for nought?" Elihu's question (35:7) reflected the one Eliphaz raised in 22:2, "Can a man be profitable to God?" The twofold issue is: Does man have an ulterior motive in serving God? Does God have an ulterior motive in dealing with man?

Elihu, like Eliphaz before him, asserted that God's sovereignty makes him completely independent of man. Therefore he is not affected by man's sins or his righteousness (35:1–8).

Does God reward a man for his goodness? Is God unaffected by man's sins and righteousness? Strahan believed that Elihu was wrong. "He [Elihu] does not realise that God does gain what He desires most by the goodness of men, and loses what He most loves by their evil." [4]

Turning from the thought of the sovereignty of God, Elihu took up the issue of God's silence. He said that men cry out for help against the oppressor, but God does not answer because their cry is empty (35:13). They do not cry to God their Maker, "who gives songs in the night" (35:10). Now, if God remains silent in the face of the misdirected cry of the oppressed, how much less likely was God to answer Job when he cried out against God and waited almost daringly for God to answer against him (35:14).

With the picture of Job's challenge to God and his waiting for God to answer him, the book seems to be building again toward the climax in which God answered Job.

God Is Just and Great (36:1 to 37:24)

Elihu was still bent on defending God against Job's charges. In this last speech Elihu summoned "his knowledge from afar" and claimed to be one who was "perfect in knowledge" (36:3–4). He said that God's justice can be seen in his treatment of man. God punishes the wicked and saves the righteous (36:6–7; compare Ex. 34:7). "The righteous" evidently includes transgressors who, when warned, repent, serve God, and spend the rest of their days in prosperity and pleasantness (36:8–11). But, contended Elihu, Job had refused to confess his sins. Instead he had tried to dictate to God how he should be treated (36:17–23).

More amazing to Elihu than God's rule of men is his control over nature. God's rule of nature was discussed in the dialogue by Job and his friends. They stressed the beneficent aspects of God's control of the rain and seasons whereas Job stressed the destructive forces of nature (5:9–10; 9:5–10).

Elihu, almost in anticipation of the speeches of Yahweh, recited the great acts of God in nature and was overwhelmed by his power. Elihu was impressed with how God draws up the raindrops and distils them again into rain, which he drops abundantly upon man (36:27–28). Elihu could not understand how God spreads out the clouds, sends the lightning to strike its marks, and makes the thunder crash. But he believed these are instruments of judgment and blessing.

From the autumn rains, Elihu turned to describe the winter's snow, which suspends man's labor and drives the wild beasts to their dens (37:6–10). The clouds turn round and round under God's guidance to accomplish all that he commands them on the habitable earth (37:11–12). "Whether for correction, or for his land, or for love, he causes it to happen" (37:13).

Elihu asked Job whether he could understand God's rule of nature or match God's power and skill. He asked whether Job really wanted to speak to God and risk being swallowed up by him (37:14–20).

The concluding remarks of Elihu furnish a remarkable background for the voice of God to speak from the whirlwind. The motif of the thunder being the voice of God runs throughout this last part of Elihu's speech. He declared that if men cannot look at the brightness of the sky when the wind has cleared away the clouds after the rain, how much less could men look upon the splendor and terrible majesty of God (37:21–22). God does not appear visibly. In this respect, man cannot look upon God. But although man cannot see God, he can know that God's justice is as great as his power, and that God will not violate abundant righteousness (37:23).

> Therefore men fear [worship] him;
> he does not regard any who are
> wise in their own conceit. —37:24

Elihu had had his say. He had not solved Job's problem. He had stressed God's greatness and justice. He had said that man cannot see God and that God is under no obligations to answer Job or anyone else. Man should fear God and believe in his justice. Just then the thunder of God's voice began to speak to Job.

---

1. Kelly, *op. cit.*, p. 129.
2. Anthony Towne, *Excerpts from the Diaries of the Late God* (New York: Harper and Row, 1968), pp. 11, 102.
3. John Paterson, *The Book That Is Alive,* (New York: Chas. Scribners Sons, 1954), pp. 90–91.
4. Strahan, *op. cit.*, p. 294.

10

Out of the Whirlwind

(38:1 to 42:6)

THE THUNDER of God's voice came to Job out of a whirlwind. A whirlwind or a storm was often the setting of a theophany (an appearance of God) in ancient Israel. When God appeared to Moses and the children of Israel at Sinai "there were thunders and lightnings, and a thick cloud upon the mountain, and a very loud trumpet blast . . . And the Lord came down upon Mount Sinai" (Ex. 19:16, 20). The writer of Deuteronomy quoted Moses as saying of this incident:

> And you came near and stood at the foot of the mountain, while the mountain burned with fire to the heart of heaven, wrapped in darkness, cloud, and gloom. Then the Lord spoke to you out of the midst of the fire; you heard the sound of words, but saw no form; there was only a voice.
>
> —Deuteronomy 4:11–12

To doubt that God spoke to Job in the whirlwind would be like denying that God spoke to Moses at the burning bush or to Isaiah in the Temple. Was Job expecting God to speak to him? Did Eliphaz, Bildad, Zophar, or Elihu expect God to appear to answer Job's charges? Did these other participants in the debate see the storm or hear the voice? We do not know. And it is pointless to guess.

While Job may have been somewhat surprised when God spoke to him, he was not so overwhelmed by God's presence and voice that he could not retain control of his mental and emotional faculties. Job heard God clearly and responded appropriately yet voluntarily.

What is surprising and perhaps disappointing to the modern reader is that God did not answer Job's question of why he was suffering. No explanation or apology is offered for God's allowing Job to endure great suffering. No mention is made of the heavenly council or Satan's challenge of Job's religious integrity. God has no intention of being cross-examined by man. He will ask the questions, not man.

The aim of the Yahweh (Jehovah, KJV) speeches is not to supply the intellect with answers to philosophical and theological questions; it is to resolve the spiritual problem of Job's seeming alienation from God. The wonder of these speeches is not in the answers they give but in the fact that God spoke at all. Job's friends had claimed that God had abandoned Job because of his sins. He felt that God had abandoned him unjustly, because, he contended, he had not sinned to an extent that would justify such suffering.

Then God appeared to Job while he was suffering to show him that his suffering had not separated him from God. God appeared to Job before Job repented, and before his restoration to health and prosperity. H. H. Rowley wrote: "If he had found God only after his restoration, the book would have been spiritually far inferior. It is of the essence of its message that Job found God *in* his suffering, and so found relief not *from* his misfortunes, but *in* them. God was to him now far more precious than he has ever been." [1]

> It is God who now speaks to Job; and in his teaching of men He never moves in the region of the mere understanding, but always in that of the religious life. He may remove perplexities regarding His providence and ways from men's minds, but He does not do so by the immediate communication of intellectual light, but by flushing all the channels of thought and life with a deeper

> sense of Himself. . . . This is the meaning of God's manifestation to Job out of the storm. He brings himself and His full glory near to Job, and fills his mind with such a sense of Him as he has never had before—"Now mine eye seeth thee" (ch. xliii.5). At this sight of God his heart not only quivers with an unspeakable joy, but he abhors his past thoughts of Him, and his former words, and repents in dust and ashes.[2]

In his speeches, God did not deal with Job's sufferings or their cause; he only dealt with the limits of Job's knowledge. True, Job and his friends had acknowledged God's omnipotence and omniscience, but they were also proud of their own knowledge. Each claimed to be as wise as the other, and Elihu claimed to be "perfect in knowledge" (36:4).

The concern of the Yahweh speeches seems to be Job's challenge of the justice of God as seen in his operation of the universe. Job had called aloud, "There is no justice" (19:7). Now, before a man begins to charge God with injustices in his operation of the universe, that man ought to be sure he has all the facts about the universe and about justice. In fact, before man begins to judge anyone or anything he needs perfect knowledge about that person or thing. Jesus said: "Judge not that you be not judged. . . . Why do you see the speck that is in your brother's eye, but do not notice the log that is in your own eye?" (Matt. 7:1, 3; compare Rom. 2:1; 14:10–13).

No man is justified in leveling the charge of injustice against God or a fellowman unless the whole case is known. It is evident that Job did not have all of the facts before him. In God's speeches, the wonderful panorama of creation is made to pass before Job's eyes, until he confessed that he had spoken without knowledge.

It is true that modern man may not be as baffled by some of God's questions about the operation of nature as Job was. Science has discovered at least partial answers to some of the questions God asked Job. Men have "entered into the springs of the sea" and "walked in the recesses of the deep" (38:16). They have "comprehended the expanse of the earth" (38:18), and "entered the storehouses" of the snow and hail (38:22). They know when the mountain goats bring forth their young and can observe the calving of the hinds (39:1).

But does this mean that man has arrived; that he is omniscient; that his knowledge is perfect? No, a thousand times no! Modern man still does not have sufficient knowledge to judge God's creation and operation of the universe. Man still cannot "deck himself with majesty" and take over the control of the universe (40:10–14). With all of his knowledge man cannot even operate his society and his technology without polluting himself and his environment almost to the point of self-destruction. Man's knowledge of the universe is still severely limited. Modern man who would criticize God's justice on the basis of his operation of the universe should confess with Job: "I have uttered what I did not understand, things too wonderful for me, which I did not know" (42:3).

There are two speeches of Yahweh in this section of the book, each followed by a brief response from Job. Some scholars have denied that these speeches belonged to the original book of Job—a view that is unacceptable to this writer and to many others. The second of these Yahweh speeches has often been questioned. The style may be somewhat different, and the content not as significant as other parts of Job, but there is no real reason to question the authenticity of this part of the book.

Yahweh's First Speech—The Wonders of Nature (38:1 to 39:30)

Job was addressed as a man who "darkens counsel by words" or "who clouds God's design in darkness" (38:2, NEB). God commanded him: "Gird up your loins," for battle, or for a race (38:3). God was going to ask Job some questions, which Job could not answer because his knowledge or strength was small. These questions point up the utter presumption of man to seek to contend with God. The questions serve to contrast the might of God with the inadequacies of man.

Was Job present on creation's morning "when the morning stars sang together, and all the sons of God shouted for joy"

(38:4–7)? Was it Job who caused the sea to be born and set boundaries for it so that it would not engulf the habitable earth (38:8–11)? Did Job ever command a sunrise in all its sharpness and purity—before pollution (38:12–15)? Had Job come to an understanding of the water that runs under the earth? Or, of Sheol? Could he comprehend the fulness of the earth (38:16–18)? "Declare, if you know all this," said God in verse 18.

God jibed Job a little when he said that Job should understand the mysteries of light and darkness since he must have been born before they were (38:19–21). Had Job ever been to the storehouses of the snow and hail, or to the place from which comes the wind and lightning (38:22–24)? Could Job explain how and why God would bring rain to a land where no man lived (38:25–30)? Could Job change the formation or movement of the constellations, number the clouds, or "tilt the waterskins of the heavens" (38:31–38)? Certainly Job knew who did all of this. But God's question was whether he had been present at creation to speak with knowledge of what happened.

After this brilliant review of what we call cosmology, meteorology, and astronomy, Job was asked to consider the mysteries of the animal world (38:39 to 39:30). Did Job feed the lion and the raven (38:39–41)? Did Job know about the life processes of the mountain goats and hinds (39:1–4)? Could he tame the wild ass (35:5–8)? Could he give strength to the wild ox (39:9–12), speed to the ostrich (39:13–18), majesty and spirit to the battle horse (39:19–25), instinct to the migratory hawk, and keen eyesight to the eagle (39:26–30)? These questions continued to focus Job's mind on the Almighty. "Here is the same basic conviction that characterizes the whole speech of the Lord, namely, that in the presence of the order of creation man discovers such boundaries and limits to his reason that he cannot presume to understand the ways of the Almighty, much less call him into account."[3]

Job Gives Up (40:1–5)

The Lord paused in his questioning of Job long enough to

get a preliminary response from Job. Verse 2 may be translated:

> Will he who disputes with the Almighty yield?
> Will he who reproved God answer these things?
> —40:2

Job admitted that he could not answer the Lord because he was small ("light," "insignificant"). Here, seemingly for the first time, Job saw his situation in the context of the vastness of the cosmos. He began to realize that he had spoken against God too harshly and too hastily. Therefore he vowed to remain silent: "I lay my hand on my mouth, . . . I will proceed no further" (40:4–5). Job was silent, but he was still at the halfway house. He had seen the error of criticizing God's justice, but he had not yet repented of the foolish things he had said about God in the dialogue and in his soliloquies. Humility did not come easily for Job.

God's Second Speech—Job Playing God (40:6 to 41:34)

God accused Job of playing God. Job had condemned God in order to justify himself (40:8). The Almighty never condemned Job, but asked him: "Is your arm as strong as God's, and can your voice thunder like his?" God invited Job to take over the control of the universe: pouring out his wrath, meting out judgment and punishment in just measure (40:10–13). When Job could do that, God would praise (worship) him, and Job would be his own savior (40:14).

But the truth is that Job's arm was not like God's. Job was not God. He could not even control two of God's playthings, the hippopotamus (39:15) and the crocodile (41:1). If man cannot stand before a creature, how can he stand before the Creator (41:10)? God is under obligation to no man.

> Who has given to me, that I should repay him?
> Whatever is under the whole heaven is mine.
> —41:11

It may be hard for modern man to accept the fact that God and not man is the author of man's salvation.

Job's Final Word: Reconciliation (42:1–6)

Here is the climax of the book of Job. At this point Job's silence (40:1–5) gave way to confession and repentance. Job repented, not for any sin which might have caused his suffering, but for the foolish things he had said about his own goodness and God's injustice. Once again Job recognized God's omnipotence (42:2) and his own rashness (42:3). He described his previous knowledge of God as hearsay, or secondhand. Now God had spoken to him personally and Job "saw" God. He "abhors himself," or "melts away" (42:5–6; see NEB). And Job repented. This is not to say that suddenly Job agreed with his friends' accusations and repented of some gross wickedness. It was not ethical sins of which Job was guilty. It was his own self-righteousness which caused him to sin. Job received no vindication, no public approval. He no longer sought this. Rather, Job lost himself in the will of God (42:2). He became aware of and certain of God's care of him.

Throughout the book, Job has grappled with the problem of why the righteous suffer. His friends had all of the answers and yet no satisfying answers. Then Job encountered God. And, in a sense, he still got no answers, at least not the sort he sought nor the kind we often wish he had found. Instead, he sensed God saying to him, in effect: "It is not your part to know the why of all things. Yours is to realize who I am, to believe that you can trust me in all things." Job's peace came not from answers to questions but from the realization that God was there and that he cared.

Job's problem had been alienation. His solution was reconciliation. But this reconciliation with God did not come through Job's power of goodness, but through the grace of God. Job had learned that a man may suffer the loss of all things and yet be sure of the love of God. He uttered no word of triumph. He shouted no hallelujahs. His intellectual questions had not been answered, but now he could say with Paul: "I rejoice in the Lord greatly. . . . I have learned, in whatever state I am, to be content. I know how to be abased and I know how to abound; in any and all circumstances I have learned the secret of facing plenty and hunger, abundance and want.

I can do all things in him who strengthens me" (Phil. 4:10–13).

---

1. H. H. Rowley, *Job* "The Century Bible," (London: Thomas Nelson, 1970), p. 20.
2. A. B. Davidson, *Job*, "The Cambridge Bible," (Cambridge: The University Press, 1893), p. 259.
3. Kelly, *op. cit.*, p. 145.

11

The Epilogue: Restoration

(42:7–17)

THE END OF the book of Job is similar to the beginning. The style of writing is prose. Job is presented as an extremely wealthy man with another ideal family. His daughters are the fairest in the land. He becomes an effective intercessor for those who had accused him falsely (42:9). He is restored to a place of respect and favor in the community (42:11). After his restoration Job lived another one hundred and forty years, twice the length of the average life span mentioned in Psalm 90:10. He is bowed off the stage with the simple yet satisfying conclusion, "And Job died, an old man, and full of days" (42:17).

Is this epilogue necessary? Does not the restoration of Job's wealth confirm the argument of his friends that God blesses materially those who serve him? Does it not leave the impression that if a man is right with God eveything else will turn out all right? Such a man will become rich, have an ideal family and lots of friends, and will live to a ripe old age. Many modern scholars have observed that life is seldom like that, and they argue that the epilogue detracts from the story.

H. Wheeler Robinson was one of those for whom the epilogue was unsatisfactory. He said,

> We could do without his doubled number of sheep and camels. . . . They only hide from us the central figure, tragic, majestic, noble in his struggle, but commonplace and comfortable in the last scene of all. We do not want to know about his new daughters, with their graceful names of Dove, Cassia, and Horn of Antimony; our sympathies are with the buried children of the earlier days. We would rather have left Job on his dung-heap, with faith shining the more brightly against the background of misfortunes. This is the natural attitude, except for those readers who want all tales to end happily, unlike the present tale of life.[1]

We must confess that it is possible to look at the epilogue that way. There is a sense in which it creates a problem for a modern reader. But there is another way of looking at the epilogue. Positively, the epilogue does three things: One, it brings the book to a simple and satisfying conclusion. Without the epilogue we would have been left wondering what happened to Job and his friends. Although some moderns would have preferred to have left Job on his ash heap, many others appreciate the satisfaction of knowing what finally happened to Job.

A second thing the epilogue does is to demonstrate that Job was right in maintaining his innocence and thereby showing that it is possible for a man to suffer for some reason other than for his sins. Suffering is often mysterious, but it should not rob one of his faith in God.

The epilogue also shows the possibility and even the probability of restoration. What a dark world this would be if there were no hope of a better tomorrow. Paul Scherer asserted:

> To those who think the poem is well-nigh ruined by its "happy ending," let it be said that there is restoration in this world of God; there is even reward, which in normal sequence is the result of restoration—though one must keep from attaching a too facile interpretation to

> them. To have said nothing of them would have been to misrepresent a fact of experience.[2]

Thus the book of Job ends. Job is exonerated. His trial is over; his faith is triumphant. He could have said: "I have fought the good fight, I have finished the race, I have kept the faith" (2 Tim. 4:7). He suffered bitter physical, mental, and spiritual anguish, without any sense of the presence of God, only to come out of his trials confessing that God's grace is sufficient and his will is best. If Job could have that kind of faith on the basis of a hearsay religion which was confirmed in the appearance of God out of a whirlwind, how much greater should our faith be this side of Calvary, the empty tomb, and Pentecost!

1. H. W. Robinson, *op. cit.*, p. 42.
2. *Job*, "Interpreter's Bible," Vol. 3, p. 1195.

Personal Learning Activities

CHAPTER 1

1. Name the principles of interpretation that one must consider in understanding Job. Explain one principle.
2. Name three limitations of the book of Job.
3. Is Job a drama? If not, why not?
4. Name three great truths one can gain from a study of Job.

CHAPTER 2

5. List the five adjectives used by Dr. Smith to show the character of Job.
6. In three or four sentences describe Satan as he is depicted in the book of Job.
7. What did God tell Satan he was *not* to do to Job?
8. List the afflictions that came upon Job.
9. Name Job's "miserable comforters."

CHAPTER 3

10. How does Job seem to change in attitude beginning with chapter 3?
11. How did Job feel about his birthday?
12. What questions did Job raise in chapter 3?

CHAPTER 4

13. In one or two sentences each, describe Job's three friends.
14. State the major theme of each of the three cycles of speeches.
15. Briefly summarize one of the speeches and Job's response to it.

CHAPTER 5

16. What is the major theme of the second argument in Job?
17. Comment briefly on the meaning of the following words and phrases: "witness in heaven"; "umpire"; "maintain his right"; "I know that my Redeemer lives." (See Job 16:18 to 17:2 and 19:25.)
18. Does the book of Job attempt to answer the question of why the wicked prosper and the righteous suffer?

CHAPTER 6

19. What is meant by the transcendance of God?
20. What was wrong with Eliphaz' ideas about repentance?
21. What was Job's greatest frustration about God?
22. List several of the phrases which Job used to sing of the greatness of God in 26:5–14.

CHAPTER 7

23. List the three parts of the hymn in praise of wisdom.

CHAPTER 8

24. Why is Job 31 considered an unusually great chapter?
25. Describe the oath of innocence which was required in ancient Israel on the part of one claiming to be innocent of crime.
26. List the three things Job said kept him from sinning.
27. Of what sins did Job say he was innocent (list)?
28. What was wrong with all of Job's protests of innocence? Of what was he guilty?

CHAPTER 9

29. List four things you learned about Elihu from this chapter.
30. Define "theodicy." Why is this word important in this chapter?
31. List the three stages in the development of men's understanding of the relationship of sin and suffering in the Bible (see Smith's comments).
32. What is the twofold issue in Job which is pointed up in this chapter?

CHAPTER 10

33. Did God tell Job why he was suffering?
34. What did God mean to do for Job by appearing to him?
35. What was the point of all of God's questions to Job?
36. Did God answer Job's questions? If not, what did God teach Job which solved his problem?

CHAPTER 11

37. List the three things the epilogue does.
38. What was your major understanding of Job before you studied this book?
39. Write two or three sentences to express your present understanding of the major truths of the book of Job.

Suggested Bibliography

Davidson, A. B., and Lanchester, H. C. O., *Job,* "The Cambridge Bible." Cambridge: The University Press, 1937.

Blackwood, Andrew W. Jr., *Devotional Introduction to Job.* Grand Rapids, Michigan: Baker Book House, 1959.

Ellison, H. L., *From Tragedy to Triumph.* London: The Paternoster Press, 1958.

Hulme, William E., *Dialogue in Despair, Pastoral Commentary on the Book of Job.* Nashville: Abingdon Press, 1968.

Johnson, L. D., *Out of the Whirlwind: The Message of Job.* Nashville: Broadman Press, 1971.

Kelly, Balmer H., *The Layman's Bible Commentaries,* "Ezra to Job." London: SCM Press, Ltd, 1962.

Rowley, H. H., *Job.* "The Century Bible." London: Thomas Nelson and Sons, Ltd, 1970.

Sanders, Paul S., *Twentieth Century Interpretations of the Book of Job.* Englewood Cliffs, N. J.: Prentice-Hall, Inc., 1968.

Terrien, Samuel, *Job: Poet of Existence.* Indianapolis: The Bobbs-Merrill Company, Inc., 1957.

Terrien, Samuel, and Scherer, Paul, *The Book of Job.* "The Interpreter's Bible," Volume III, New York: Abingdon Press, 1954.

Wood, James, *Job and the Human Situation.* London: Geoffrey Bles, 1966.

Yates, Kyle M. *et al. Broadman Bible Commentary,* Volume 4. Nashville: Broadman Press, 1971.

Suggested Audiovisual Materials

FILMSTRIPS:

Job: A Spiritual Pilgrim, Part One. Cathedral. 60 frames, color, manual, recording, 17 minutes. Filmstrip and manual, $7.00; recording, $3.50.

Job: A Spiritual Pilgrim, Part Two. Cathedral. 39 frames, color, manual, recording, 14 minutes. Filmstrip and manual, $7.00; recording, $3.50.

RECORDING:

The Basis of Hope. WORD. John R. Claypool. 12″, 33⅓ rpm. $4.98.

Broadman Films Presents
Job: A Study in Providence and Faith
a filmstrip
Prepared especially for use with
this book.

The New Church Study Course

THE NEW CHURCH STUDY COURSE effective in January 1970 is based on more than three years of study and design. It offers several improvements in the Church Study Course, which began in October 1959. At that time three courses previously promoted by the Sunday School Board were merged: the Sunday School Training Course, the Graded Training Union Study Course, and the Church Music Training Course. Principles and methods books of the Woman's Missionary Union and the Brotherhood Commission were added in October 1961 and January 1967 respectively.

The New Church Study Course offers increased flexibility in meeting the needs of Southern Baptists. It provides courses of varying length and difficulty, varied formats and types of course materials, additional types of credit, and improved organization of courses.

The New Church Study Course consists of two types of courses: Christian Development Courses for all church members, and Christian Leadership Courses for church leaders. Courses are organized into subject areas.

The purpose of the Christian Development Courses is to provide study which will help church members grow toward maturity in Christian living and competence in Christian service. These courses offer more comprehensive, advanced, and varied learning experiences in subject areas of a church's educational program than can be provided through curriculum periodicals. Tests and exercises, credits, and diplomas of achievement which help church members measure their progress in developing needed knowledge, understanding, and skills are included in some courses. Units of instruction are provided for Preschoolers and Children. These are designed to reinforce foundational learnings. Materials which churches may use in recognizing the participation of Children in these units are available from the Baptist Book Stores.

The Christian Leadership Courses provide a comprehensive series of courses organized into subject areas dealing with knowledge, understandings, and skills needed for effective church leadership. Tests and exercises, credits and diplomas to help leaders measure their growth in leadership ability are included in some courses. The Christian Leadership Courses are the primary source for leadership training materials prepared by the agencies cooperating in the New Church Study Course.

Courses of both types are designed to be effective for individual and class study. Learning aids, study guides, and teaching guides are available for some courses. Credits are granted to Youth and Adults for reading, individual study, and class study.

The New Church Study Course is promoted by the Sunday School Board, 127 Ninth Avenue, North, Nashville, Tennessee 37203, through the departments in the Education Division; by the Woman's Missionary Union, 600 North Twentieth Street, Birmingham, Alabama 35203; by the Brotherhood Commission, 1548 Poplar Avenue, Memphis, Tennessee 38104; and by the respective departments in the state conventions affiliated with the Southern Baptist Convention.

A record of all credits and diplomas earned should be maintained in each church.

Detailed information about the course, the system of credits and diplomas, and the keeping of records is available from the agencies listed above.

Forms for keeping records may be ordered from any Baptist Book Store.

Requirements for Credit

THIS BOOK is the text for course 3210 of subject area Biblical Revelation of the New Church Study Course. If credit is desired for this course through class study, individual study, or reading, the following requirements must be met:

I. CLASSWORK

1. This course is designed for seven and one-half (7½) hours of class study and carries three credits for such usage. If the course is studied in a class setting of less than seven and one-half (7½) hours, the following criteria apply:
   (1) Five (5) class hours—two (2) credits
   (2) Two and one-half class hours—one (1) credit
   The teacher will indicate the length of the class and the number of credits to be granted on Form 151, Request for Course Credit. For courses in which laboratory experience or practice is desirable, two hours of such guided experience may be substituted as one hour of class time, provided at least half of the required hours are actually spent in classwork.
2. A class member who attends all class sessions and completes the reading of the book as directed by the teacher will not be required to do any written work for credit.
3. A class member who is absent from one or more sessions must complete the required exercises or questions in the "Personal Learning Activities" section on all chapters he misses. In such a case, he must turn in his paper by the date

the teacher sets (usually within ten days following the last class). Also, he must certify that he has read the book.

4. The teacher should request an award for himself. A person who teaches a course for youth or adults (in any subject area) will be granted the same number of credits as class members. The teacher of an approved unit of study for preschoolers and children will be granted two credits in course 6299 in subject area 62. Request award by using Form 151.
5. The director of church training, or the person designated by the church, should complete Form 151, Request for Course Credit, and forward it after completion of the class to the Church Study Course Awards Office, 127 Ninth Avenue, North, Nashville, Tennessee 37203.

II. Individual Study

1. A person who wishes to complete this course without attending class sessions may receive full credit by certifying that he has read the book and by completing all exercises or questions in the "Personal Learning Activities" section.
2. Students may find profit in studying the text together, but individual papers are required. Carbon copies or duplicates of the answers cannot be accepted.
3. The work required for individual study credit should be turned in for checking to the director of church training or the person designated by the church to administer the New Church Study Course. The form entitled "Request for Course Credit" (Form 151) must be used in requesting these awards. It is to be forwarded by the director of church training or the person designated by the church to the Church Study Course Awards Office, 127 Ninth Avenue, North, Nashville, Tennessee 37203.

III. Reading Credit

1. A person may receive one credit toward the diploma on which he is working by reading this book.
2. Upon completion of the reading, he must complete Form 151, Request for Course Credit. He should give the completed form to the director of church training or to the person designated by his church to be responsible for administering the New Church Study Course.
3. The director of church training or the person designated by the church will see that the request is completed, signed,

and forwarded to the Church Study Course Awards Office, 127 Ninth Avenue, North, Nashville, Tennessee 37203.

IV. Awards and Records

Two copies of the course credit award form will be sent by the Study Course Awards Office to the church. One copy should be filed in the church training record and the other given to the individual.